LYBLÁC
ANGLO SAXON WITCHCRAFT

BY WULFEAGE

CAPALL BANN PUBLISHING

www.capallbann.co.uk

LYBLÁC
ANGLO SAXON WITCHCRAFT

ISBN 186163 287 8
ISBN 13 9781861632876

Cover design by HR Design
www.hr-design.co.uk

Published by:

Capall Bann Publishing
Auton Farm
Milverton
Somerset
TA4 1NE

To my wife Julie without whom I wouldn't have got far at all, so my eternal thanks go to you.

Grateful thanks must go to Ingwulf & Mægwyn (Lee & Tracy Billington) for their help and support in this venture.

Also Wulfcwen (Paula) for your help and assistance.

And especially to Dr Raymond Buckland who has been an inspiration to me

Thank you all.

Wulfeage

Ealdormann & Founder of the Lyblác high witan.

About the author

Wulfeage (pronounced Wolf-ay-guh) was born to parents Leonard & Lillian Percival in a caravan upon Wychbury hill, Hagley, Worcestershire on the 14th day of July in 1958. From an early age he had felt and experienced the forces of magic and mystery growing up as he did surrounded by folklore and spell-craft. Destined at first to walk another path he stumbled upon a book in 1976 written by Raymond Buckland which was namely "*The Complete book of Saxon Witchcraft*". The style, equality and down to earth content of the book clicked straight away with Wulfeage (then known as Sean Percival) the book coupled with his already strong connection to Witchcraft and the northern pantheon of gods set him firmly along a rewarding path. A path full of such promise, of love and of light in a tradition equal and well rounded which is known today as Seax Wica.

Wulfeage reached the heights of becoming initiated as High priest of the coven of the spiral Seax and later ordained taking on positions such as 1st Eorl of the Seax high Witan and indeed at some stages worked diligently for the pagan community as a whole working as general secretary and chairman of a few pagan organisations. Whilst for the most part very content Wulfeage felt a longing from within himself and the craft in general. He felt that this need that was simultaneously developing from within the Pagan community as a whole was taking the form of once more turning away from the elitist Witchy clubs as it did in the 60`s and was rearing its head above the mire showing a yearning for a more solid, equal and ancestral connection to our Witchcraft heritage and roots. Wulfeage started to delve ever deeper into the magical crafts and traditions of Wicca/Witchcraft, and although in some ways connections could be made throughout the magical world as they have done so many times before, indeed he soon found that the practice of our ancestors from the northern nations held too many coincidences for

Witchcraft in general not to be of Anglo Saxon, English and northern origins. So after speaking to a well known occultist and writer he destined himself to seek a somewhat overlooked tradition and its associations to our English occult and heathen past which indeed he now believes as we of the Lyblác do that it is the very foundations of Wicce/Wiccercræft and the Earth Mother.

Enter Lyblác Anglo Saxon Witchcraft.

Mægwyn

Lybbestre/Priestess

Billingswolf Coven

Introduction by Raymond Buckland

In 1973 I published *The Tree: The Complete Book of Saxon Witchcraft* (reissued by Red Wheel/Weiser in 2005 as *Buckland's Book of Saxon Witchcraft*). At the time it was the first book to explore Wicca from a Solitary perspective. It came into print less then twenty years after Gerald Gardner's ground-breaking book Witchcraft Today, which was the very first to delineate Witchcraft as "The Old Religion." I had been initiated by Gardner's High Priestess in late 1963 but a decade later I had become uncomfortable with certain aspects, both of that tradition and of the way it was being administered by some coven leaders. I therefore broke away and founded my own tradition; that of Seax-Wica.

Seax-Wica was never meant to be a reconstruction of the ancient Saxon ways of working witchcraft, nor did it claim unbroken lineage from those times. It was simply a new "tradition", with brand new rituals, but built on a foundation, as it were, of Saxon beliefs. The make-up of it was such that it drew many Seekers to it. There were innovative aspects, such as the ability to Self-Initiate, the reality of Solitary practice, and the democratic construction of covens which precluded ego-trips and power-plays which had become prevalent in many other traditions.

Over the years the Seax-Wica tradition has spread around the world, with both covens and Solitaries in a wide variety of countries. But also over the years, a need has grown among some for a more direct connection with the actual Saxon beliefs and practices. This is fine and as it should be, for no religion should stagnate and the greater variety it can offer, the greater attraction it has for a wide variety of people. Individual groups have adapted what I originally presented, to suit their needs . . . something I always encouraged. Now Wulfeage has gone a step farther and presented a new perspective with *Lyblác – Anglo-Saxon Witchcraft*. In this work, he has introduced more Anglo-Saxon lore and magical practice. As Wulfeage points out, it is "near impossible to re-create the exact rituals of a thousand years ago," but what he has accomplished is to give us the very feel and flavour of what those rituals must have been like. Lyblác (Lybblác, or Lybbcræft) was the ancient Anglo Saxon term and perhaps it's time to revive it. This book is an excellent tool to do that.

Contents

Foreword 13
History 15
Beliefs 19
Language & Pronunciation 20
Coincidence or Heritage 22
The Gods 26
Woden 26
Freya/Frigg/Frigga 28
Thunar/†unor 30
Eostre/Ostara 31
Nerthus/Erca (Eorðan mòdor) 32
Ing (Ingui Fréa) 34
Hel (Goddess of Death) 35
Seaxneat (God Ancestor of the English Saxons) 37
Other beings 38
Elves 39
Deofol 39
Draca 39
Dweorg 40
Fægerfolc 40
Fetch 40
Fifel - Grendel 40
Gast 41
Ent 41
Puccel 41
Scucca 41
Wights 42
Lyblac elements 43
North (Ice) 44
South (Fire) 45
East (Air) 46
West (Water) 47
Earth (Erce) 48
A New Name 50
Titles & Names 50
Naming Rite 51

Altar & Dress 55
The Circle 57
Consecration 59
    Consecration rite 60
Affirmation of the Hearth 63
    Affirmation of the Hearth 63
    The Lyblac Call 65
Ale & Bread 70
Seal the Hearth 73
Lyblac Oath 75
Festivals 77
    Yule 77
    Lyblac New Year 81
    Mother's night 83
    Solmonath 84
    Hreðmona~ 87
    (Hrethmonath/Spring Equinox) 87
    Eostremonath 89
    Thrimilci 90
    Litha 94
    Haerfestmonath 97
    Blotmonath 101
    Full Moon 102
Lybcraeft - Skills involved in the use of plants for magic and witchcraft 105
Tools of the trade 113
    Laecseax (The Magical blade) 114
    Pocca aerende (Bag/pouch/pocket of messages) 115
    The Fates 116
    The Key 117
    Witch's staff 118
Galdorsang (Magical songs) 120
    Song of the fates 120
    Song of enchantment 121
    Wyrtgaldor 121
    The Smiðsang 122
Magic from the well of Wyrde (The Mothers) 124
Spoken/Written charms 126
    To banish illness 126
    Charm against Love/Sexual bewitchments 127
    Good fortune 128
Blessing the mead 130
    To get a Lover 131
Of Enchantments 134

To get someone to fall in love with you: 134
To turn a barren womb fertile 135
Charm against an enemy 138
A charm for confidence 139
A charm against those who disgrace & are dishonourable 140
Wet the "New born" (waeten ∂aet niwgeboren) 142
Appeasing spirits (gast geswefian) 144
House Wights 144
Land Wights 145
Summoning (abannan) 147
Life Path (bladweg) 148
To gain Success (geblaedfaestnes habben) 149
Gastboda (Spirit messenger) 151
Harii/Wuotanes her 153
Sending the Hammer (Homergaest) 158
Making a Lyblac Staff 160
Acquiring the wood 160
Staff Symbolism 161
Creating your work of Art 162
Runes 167
Supplemental A. S. runes: 217
Rune Spreads 227
North Star spread 227
Hammer spread 229
Past, Present & Future spread 230
Goddess reading 231
Reading the Runes 233
Ercen Oracle 235
Hand-Fasting 238
Lyblac Hand-fasting rite 240
Acknowledgments/ Bibliography 252

Foreword

Some years ago whilst talking with a prominent writer and occultist the conversation came around to the subject of the re-release of one of his books. He told me that his work first published in 1974 could maybe do with a little infusion of more Anglo-Saxon lore than in its present form. So I began to research the subject to see what could be done to redress the situation. It soon became apparent whilst delving deeper into our Anglo-Saxon past that not only were there prominent Witches a thousand years ago but they were known as the Lyblác. As I peered into the depths of English history I came to the conclusion that it was they who could well be the roots of modern day Wicca and of course our magical heritage known as Witchcraft. Their story had been altogether forgotten and seemingly omitted from any of our present day Witchcraft traditions or so some would have us think? But whether anyone could call it divine intervention or shear coincidence that I just happened to be there and talk with the author at that time I do not know? But what was clearly evident to me about the whole episode was that I would now be embarking upon a journey, a journey of discovery that would revive our ancestors the Lyblác and show the reality of Wicca and our long, long history of Anglo Saxon Witchcraft in England.

As anyone can easily see for themselves, so many things that are associated with the practice of Lyblác Witchcraft a thousand years ago, have almost certainly been adopted and are now used in the modern workings of Wicca and Witchcraft. Whether it is festivals, tools charms or even language there are just too many similarities and occurrences that were used by our ancestors and carbon copied by us today that just cannot be termed mere coincidence.

From the Anglo-Saxon word for Witch "Wicca" (pro- Witch-uh) to the Cytel/Kettle the Lyblác "Cauldron" from elf charms to the mass of herbal magic and remedies still used today. There are so many, many things from our A.S past that have stood the test of time and are ingrained within our Pagan psyche! All of which are just waiting to be re-discovered for what they truly are. Let us journey ever onward in a quest for the truth and the magical and spiritual knowledge bestowed to us by those that came before.

As many will know it is near impossible to re-create the exact rituals of a thousand years ago, all that can be done is that we use whatever knowledge we have in an attempt to capture some of that magical essence that coloured the Witchcraft of Anglo Saxon England. I have embarked upon that journey; I have used all that I could glean from every source available to re-create a tradition worthy of its name. I have opened myself up to the earth mother; I have invited the gods of my ancestors to welcome me as they did my forebears. I have embraced the path of truth and honour and have enjoyed the fruits of that labour. So now I invite you to walk with me. We can delve into the mists of time, look back into the realms of Lyblác Anglo Saxon Witchcraft we can take whatever we need from our ancestral paths in an attempt to grow and move forward with knowledge, love and light. We can create and re-create our own paths from the embers of ancient fires embracing the welcomed gifts of our ancestors that should serve to ensure a solid, vibrant magical and mystical future for us all.

Ingár Wulfeage. June 2004

History

Many misconceptions surround the history and origins of our Anglo-Saxon past and even the widely perceived notion held today that England was and is the only country to bear that name is in fact wrong! The origin of our merry old England lie in the Baltic nations of northern Europe, the first England (Anglia/Engla Land) was situated in what we now would call southern Denmark. It would take various Germanic tribes and many, many years to eventually form the nation that sports that name today. When the Romans left England's shores they left behind a power vacuum, there were masses of fertile and productive land with no real united army to rule it. Before the evacuation of Roman troops certain Kings and leaders paid much gold and silver to hoards of Germanic warriors to protect and police the wilds of this forming land.

It was a foregone conclusion that as the Roman invaders left the migrating protectors would stay and make their homes where they had fought, lived and loved for the last however many years secure in the knowledge that they were wanted. There is no actual archaeological proof anyway that any "Bloody Invasion" of Britain ever took place by the Saxons, Jutes. Frisians and Angli. No evidence of sackings or burnt villages or any mass graves containing Romano-Celtic-Britain's slain at that time. The facts are that the northern tribes had no need to ravage and pillage their way into power because they mixed freely with the populous taking wives and land and integrating themselves into the then diminishing Celtic-Romano-British way of life. One thing that is for certain though and can not be denied is that with the migration of the northern tribes it brought about a rich and vibrant culture of beliefs, magic and gods. The outcome of this mixing being a welcome cultural exchange that slowly percolated through British society eventually coming together over many years to form what we now know as the Anglo Saxon religion of Lyblác and almost certainly the origins of Witchcraft itself.

Tacitus describes the English as worshippers of Terra Mater the Earth Mother Nerthus he tells of how they believed that she regularly intervened in the affairs of humankind. Going on to explain about a consecrated island and sacred grove where a veiled effigy of Nerthus was placed upon a sanctified wagon. The wagon or wain was driven through the villages with only the main Priest allowed to look upon the effigy Tacitus goes on to state that lay people or ordinary folk were under pain of death should they see or gods forbid even touch the goddess. So the English at least saw the earth as a female entity and that she as "The" goddess was the mother of all humankind.

The English also worshipped Ing as the god of fertility and the male aspect to the female aspect of Nerthus. Ing sent the sunshine and life giving rains needed to nourish the earth mother so abundance and plenty could be harvested. The northern tribes of Europe at first kept their former allegiances and tribal links creating the kingdoms who's names can still be seen today as in Mercia (middle England) Wessex (west Saxons) Sussex (south Saxons) Kent, East Anglia and Northumberland. It is said that the Jutes Hengest & Horsa in the year 449 began the first major landings in southern Britain when they came to take land as payment for their mercenary duties performed whilst saving the Celts from the Picts.

The facts are though that as early as 364 Saxons had been migrating to these islands so it is easily concluded that well over 1500 years ago Germanic peoples were settling in Britain as warriors who had been invited and welcomed and not as invaders.

The burgeoning Anglo Saxon nation held blood ties very dear and to them kinship meant everything. The unions formed, won and inherited gave rise to an institution that is still the envy of the world today and that being namely the British Parliament! Have you ever wondered why Pagans of today call their meetings moots? The origins of this word are found in A.S. English i.e. *Witangemót* Meaning: meeting of the wise men or meeting of a national council. *Gemótmann* = Speaker, Counsellor. *Gemótstede* = official meeting place. The Witan of our forebears itself, acted as advisory body and council to the king in much the same way as is now the case in modern Great Britain. It extolled the attributes of equity, working together and the love of freedom, in some cases even being used to vote the King into power, components all of which have aspired many and is an Anglo Saxon heritage and legacy that we can all be very proud of.

The word *Lybb* in old English means charm, drug or magical substance. The word *Lác* means a gift, an offering, also to sacrifice and booty. Putting together both words as our forefathers did you have the Lybläc. These cunning people who over a thousand years ago possessed the gifts of magical knowledge and of Witchcraft through herbs, charms and all manner of strange substances, also had direct connections to our ancient gods. The Lybläc were of such notoriety that specific laws were made by Kings and high born men, take for instance King Edmund 1st 939-946 A.D. who introduced a direct law against them stating:

"*Those who swear falsely and are Lybläc let them be forever cast out of all commission with God, unless they turn to right repentance.*"

Again King Athelstan 924-939 A.D. before him stating in his laws on Witchcrafts:

"*And we have ordained respecting witch-crafts, and lyblács, and morthdaeds: if any one should be thereby killed, and he could not deny it, that he be liable in his life. But if he will deny it, and at threefold ordeal shall be guilty; that he be 120 days in prison: and after that let kindred take him out, and give to the king 120 shillings, and pay the wer to his kindred, and enter into borh for him, that he evermore desist from the like.*"

The Laws of Alfred, Guthrum, and Edward the Elder :

If Witches (lyblács) *or diviners be found let them be driven from the country or let them totally perish within the country, unless they desist.*

Clearly the "cunning people" from the villages and heaths were revered by the locals for their healing and magical crafts but also at the same time loathed by church and lawmakers alike for their ability to serve the people without repression or guilt.

The Anglo-Saxon laws of the time make definite distinctions between heathen practices and those of Lyblác Witchcraft. Heathen practice being tolerated much longer than that of the Lyblác. Although some may say that Witchcraft itself is a much older and earlier tradition (as wrongful interpretations have been made so many times over so many years with regards to its practices) we can see an example of this by reading one such "Interpretation" of Exodus 22:18 which states:

"Thou shalt not suffer a Witch to live."

The verse however does not tell the whole truth! The word with which the verse associates as the meaning of "Witch" is "*kashaph*" and in fact actually means poisoner or those who kill by poisoning. The only connection it can have with "Wiccercræft" is the use of baneful herbs with which if one were not proficient enough in their use they could easily kill, so the connection was made and the wrong translation added and the rest is history as they say. The verse should actually read:

"Thou shalt not suffer a poisoner to live."

and has nothing to do with Lybläc Anglo Saxon Witchcraft or any Witchcraft for that matter but served to "rally" some against solely honourable and well intentioned practitioners of a developing magical craft, that has lead us all to the point at which we find ourselves today.

Beliefs

Unlike the Wiccans of today the Anglo Saxon Lybläc did not worship a god and a goddess but would have used many of the Teutonic Pantheon. Some may even have used Roman and Celtic versions of an ever abundant wealth of godly choice and could call upon many spiritual forces to do there bidding and grant favours. Our Witch ancestors believed strict observances not to "Anger" the gods and spirits that shared their existence and sought to appease such deities with respect and consideration, paying homage to what was known as the worship of their own ancestors, their kith and kin.

They sought council with their gods; they sought guidance, discipline and nourishment. They also sought magical knowledge with which to ease the suffering of those less fortunate, and the granting of such ways with which they could bind them all together so they all could see the light of the next and future blossoming years. Harmony with their world was the order of the day everything had a "life force" a spirit and a purpose. Honour, truth and above all allegiance governed their lives.

They cherished and respected nature and used their magic in harmony and unison with the earth and gods alike. They served their brothers, sisters and their gods with a view that togetherness and the harmonious family was the key to blood and tribal advancement, equality, standing and worldly success.

Language & Pronunciation

We do not know exactly how an Anglo-Saxon would sound as no one has been around that long to hear it spoken! But there are very many clues as to how it actually sounded. We have to wade through the obvious hindrances such as regional accents and the placement of words differently to each other in any given sentence as in poetic verse but the following guide is generally thought to be the accepted form of articulation.

Letters	Short	Long
a	as in bud - b-er-d b-ird (dialect south UK)	as in lard -car
æ/œ	as in sad	as in gas
e	as in led	as in frayed
i	as in lid	as in lead
o	as in body	as in hoard
u	as in dull	as in cool
C = K/Ch	not sounded as an "S" before i & e It sounded more like the "C" in cool	cirlic = charlock cinn = chin

f	as in fade however when "f" is situated in the middle of a word its sound becomes that of "v" as in seven/seofon	as in gruff
g	as in game/hag	before e or i, it is a "y" as in year
h	Normal English sound As in home/fright	
Q = cw	as in quit	as in queen/cwen
y	ae/æ the sound "i" with rounded lips	
s	As in size (both s& z) combined with "c" it becomes the "sh" as in shop	as in stress
Th = ö & þ	as in thought/brother	as in path

OE Consonant clusters

cn	kn as in fright	
fn	fn as in fnésan/to sneeze	
gn	gn as in gnæt/gnat/midge	
hl	hl as in hlec/leaky	
hn	hn as in hlùd/loud	
hr	hr as in hræfen/raven	
hw	hw as in hwá/who	
wl	wl as in wlacu/lukewarm	
wr	wr as in wrang/wrong	
ea	as in fed eác/eke	as in fade
eo	like the above with emphasis more on the "o" sound	
ie	Like the sound "cleared" ..variants	
Io	like the above with emphasis more on the "o" sound	

The length of long vowels is printed as [´] above the letters as in á.

Coincidence or Heritage

No matter what anybody could say about the theories as to the origins of Wicca/Witchcraft, it is easy for anyone to read through the masses of research and various translations of historical Anglo-Saxon/ Roman texts, to see with their own eyes the overwhelming evidence that the "craft of the wise" has definitely got its roots firmly planted in Anglo Saxon England.

Here are just a few of the "facts" that many seem to pretend are "Coincidences" Why? For that one you will have to make up your own mind but, taken individually the so-called "coincidences" which one could align to other similar practices throughout the ancient world, were all part and parcel of the Witchcraft practices collectively throughout Saxon England. To discount that fact is seen as to be afraid of their power and importance concerning the history and beginnings/origins of Witchcraft.

Modern Wicca/ Witchcraft	Anglo Saxon Lybléc
The circle	A representation of Brossingamene Freya`s necklace that symbolises Light over darkness. Birth, death and re-birth.
The Athame	The Laecseax used by the Lybléc for the preparation of magical herbs & substances.
The staff	Used as a badge of office by Witches also used to transcend the worlds
The broom/besom	The staff disguised with birch twigs because of Christian persecution. The

	first public house sign for ale and charms planted up side down on a pile of rocks outside the Witch's home as a "The Witch is open for business" signal.
Flying	A mixture of the staff and broom used to transcend the worlds.
The Familiar	Known as a "Fetch" or guardian spirit, many times in the form of an animal.
Charms and spells	Too many to mention from love magic to protection, from healing to the causing of death etc.
Cords	Red cords used extensively to bind magical energies.
Elements/Quarters	North=Ice. East=Air. South=Fire. West=Water and the Earth=Nerthus the mother as the fifth element.
Cardinal/compass points	The four dwarfs/dwarves Nordri (North) Sudri (South) Austri (East) Vestri (West) In Northern creation mythology they held the four corners of the sky made from the skull of Ymir.
Magical Herbalism	A wealth of Leechcraft/Lacnunga.
Triple Goddess	The Norns/Nornir. The three sisters that weave the web of fate for human-kind. Fate, Necessity and future.

The Earth Mother	Nerthus/Erce hailed as the most important goddess of all and the mother of all humankind.
Witch's Pouch	Pocca ærenda the bag/pouch used by Anglo Saxon Witches to hold many magical items and found in many A.S graves throughout England.
Crystals/Crystal ball	The Lyblác would use various stones especially black and white and rounded Thunderstones, also holed Amber. Clear quartz was found inside silver boxes. Rounded clear quarts have been found in numerous A.S. graves. They were placed in silver boxes and used for healing, divination and for harnessing the power of the sun.
Cauldron	The cytel/kettle used for the preparation of potions and magical substances.
Chalice/ceremonial drinking vessel	The drinking horn that represented the strength of the beast (Aurochs) but also represented the male and female energies.
Wicca	Wicca = Wicha. Wicce = Wichuh Witchcraft + Wiccacraeft = Lyblác (cc in old English is pronounced ch)
Black cats	Freya`s wagon was pulled through the skies by black cats. Also the Priesthood of Ing used cats as their familiars.

Sacred grove	The grove was the temple of the Anglo Saxons, built in a circle made out of wooden beams adorned with animal heads.
The Eight sabbats	Yule — Geol Imbolc — Solmonath Spring equinox — Hrethmonath Beltane — Thrimilci Mid summer — Litha Lughnasadh — Weodmonath Autumn equinox — Haerfestmonath Samhain — Blotmonath.
Ostara	The English extensively worshipped the Goddess Eostre. The month for April was known as Eostremonath and she was seen as the Bringer of summer.
Pagan Moots	The word comes from the A.S word for the meeting of the wise men Witangemót also Mót meaning assembly, court, council and society.
Moon rites	Anglo Saxons always held their rites on the next available full moon, indeed all their months also started at this time.
Working magic at a Crossroads magic.	Extensively noted that in A.S. times a crossroads was the place to perform
Tying the knot/ handfasting	Tying the knot in hand fasting ceremonies was used by our Anglo Saxon forebears. This was eventually replaced by the two rings that are exchanged by the bride & groom today.

The Gods

Woden

A God of fury, a God of magick, a God of death and a God of poetry his name literally means inspiration and god of the wild hunt! Shaman and shape-shifter Woden is the God that won the runes for mankind and of course for the Gods.

"I trust that I hung
on the windy tree
swung there nights of nine
deeply slashed with a blade
bloodied by Woden
myself an offering to myself
and knotted to that mighty tree
that no man knows to what place the roots run.

No one gave me bread
No one stilled my thirst,
searchingly into the depths I peered
eagerly snatching the runes with a strident cry
And then I fell into a dizzied faint!

Wellbeing I won and wisdom too,
and grew and rejoiced in my growth.
From a word I advanced to a word
From a deed towards another deed."

Stanzas 138, 139,141.

Often called the "one eyed lord" Woden, would move amongst his people sometimes even disguised as a woman, more often than not though he would appear as an old man with long white hair and beard to match leaning upon a strong staff sporting a large brimmed hat and long grey cloak.

Noted by the Romans in the 1st century Woden was afforded special significance by the Teutonic tribes and described as being a Germanic form of "Mercurius" (The god Mercury). Hugin and Munin two black ravens who's names mean "Thought" and "Memory" accompany Woden and are charged with flying to the far and wide reaches of the worlds to find out the deeds of mankind and of the Gods .

The Lord Woden is also depicted with two companion wolves Geri & Freki they are a representation of intelligence, bravery and the protection of the pack. They also reveal that through Woden`s control over these wolves that it is possible to conquer the darker side of his and our own savage and primeval nature.

DAY: Wednesday (O.E.. Wodnes-daeg)

Element: Air

Rune: ᚨ Language, Transformation, persuasion.

Tree: Ash

The God Woden can be invoked for:

Protection. Courage, Magick, Runic practices, Self awareness, Courage, Death issues, Self-sacrifice, Language/the mind/communication.

Freya/Frigg/Frigga

Although it is widely thought that, the Goddess Freya could also be the Goddess Frigg/Frigga it still goes without saying that she has always been known as the loveliest of all the Goddesses. Consort to Woden she is the bearer of the light of *Brosingamene the sacred necklace stolen by Loki and returned to her from the underworld. She is a powerful Goddess of life, death and re-birth. Freya the deity of fertility, love & nature is seen as the ultimate guardian without whom there would be no light only eternal darkness and misery throughout the world. She is our shinning Lady who embodies the balance and harmony of all the worlds. For as night has day, heat has cold and death has life Freya is the feminine element to the masculinity of our Lord Woden.

Freya just like Frigg is a Goddess of the matronly virtues and of childbirth, she is noted to be the ultimate midwife and mother so to speak. Her connection to Frigg can also be seen in the fact that both Goddesses are said to be able to turn themselves into Falcons, and both are revered as Queens of the heavens. Their symbol is the Boar Hildisvini (Battle-Swine) and she has authority over half of those slain in battle. Freya has two winged cats that are said to pull her carriage through the sky. She is also the mistress of Seidh, which refers to her various kinds of magical practice, and power, which include prophecy and divination. Freya taught the mystery, practice and magical techniques of Seidh to our Lord Woden/Odin which may have enabled him to shape-shift into whomever or whatever form he pleased. Although accounts in Anglo Saxon England are scarce where Freya is concerned she was definitely a Saxon deity, worshipped widely by the northern Saxon tribes.

A stone on which an inverted heart has been carved may represent the Goddess upon the Altar. The heart, being her symbol that shows the breasts or buttocks of womanly form which later on became the up-turned Christianised badge represent the heart.

Day: Friday (O.E. Frige-dæg)

Element: Air & Fire

Rune: ᛗ Intelligence. Magical knowledge. ᛒ Life, Beauty.

Tree: Apple.

* Brosingamene Freya`s necklace that had been stolen by Loki was returned to her with the help of Heimdal.

The Goddess Freya can be invoked for:

Magick, Children & Childbirth, Passion/Love, All forms of Fertility, Beauty, Home & Family, Battle, Protection.

Thunar/Þunor

Son of the Earth and of Odin, Thunar the sky God is best known as a god of the common people and a protector of all the Gods. His symbol the hammer Mjöllnir is wide spread throughout the countries of Northern Europe and he was always seen as a practical problem solving deity being often known as "Deep thinker". A fighter of giants and protector of Mother Earth without a doubt Thunar is able to summon great strength and rage when all else fails. He is seen moving throughout the skies on a wagon pulled by two goats named Tanngnjóstr and Tanngrísnir.

His great physique, red hair and the wielding of the great Mjöllnir are impressive signs of his might. If your heart is sincere and your prayers honest and true? Call upon Thunar God of the hammer to unleash the power of the storm.

Day: Thursday (O.E. ðunres-dæg)

Element: Air

Rune: ᚦ Organisation. Harmony through strength. Foresight. Protection.

Tree: Rowan. Leek

The God Thunar can be invoked for:

Justice, Protection, Marriage, Purification, Potential, strength, The Greater good, Cunning, Problem solving, Oaths.

Eostre/Ostara

A goddess of the growing light of the dawn and the awakening of the year she is a deity of promise and of our past deeds. Her symbol is the Sun wheel seen decorating "Hot cross buns" of Easter time which in turn are representations of the rising spring Sunshine as it emerges into the heavens.

At the festival of Eostre, fresh water would be drawn to symbolically nourish the plants. These magical well waters also symbolised the morning dew that catch the morning rays of the sun and shine like diamonds gifted to us by the Goddess herself. Fertility plays a major role in the symbology of Eostre; eggs were rolled down the hillsides to show the suns journey as it traversed the skies from dawn to dusk. The Hare also played a prevalent part at that time as it does today and denoted the essence of life itself which along with its obvious fertility connotations are still potent connections to this very day.

Month: April/Easter (O.E. Eostra)

Element: Earth, Air, Fire & Water.

Rune: ᚨ Deep gestation. Activation.

The Goddess Eostra can be invoked for:

Growth, Fertility, Enlightenment, New life, New ventures, Fruition, Promise, Hope, Just deserts, Ideas,

Nerthus/Erca (Eorðan mòdor)

Goddess of the fruitful earth "The Mother" is one of the oldest known Teutonic deities. Mother to Thunar she is known as Nerthus and Erca and was originally worshipped by a Priesthood who would cover her effigy and keep her away from prying eyes. They kept the effigy on a sacred island, which would only be tended by Priesthood of men. On certain feast days her veiled statue would be carried from the island, placed upon a wagon and drawn through the villages by mighty oxen. At the time of this procession it was ordained that all weapons should be hidden from view and a human sacrifice was made should the wrong person look upon the Goddess. Each year Nerthus would be crowned as Queen of the Harvest and her crown was always made using the last harvested sheaf of grain interwoven with flowers and placed upon her head before she was paraded for all to see.

Part of an Anglo-Saxon prayer about her reads:

Hal wes þu, folde, fira modor
Beo þu growende on godes fæþme,
fodre gefylled firum to nytte.

One translation is:

Hale this soil, Mankind's mother.
Be growing within Gods outstretched arms
Filled of food, joyous to care.

Nerthus is the ultimate goddess of fertility and strength; she was seen as a strong, powerful female form that brought gifts of fruitfulness and abundance to the world and to all of human kind. In her honour cakes were made from milk, water and the flour of every available grain which when baked were placed not only upon her Altar but laid within the first ploughed furrow of every farm to act as a symbolic coupling of the god and the goddess. This symbolic act of fertilisation and penetration by the God was performed to insure a bounteous harvest and the continued success of the tribe. Her symbol is a veiled oblong stone crowned with a head dress of flowers and grain.

Element: Earth

Rune: ᛒ Birth, Liberation. ᚷ Gift, Sacrifice.

Tree: Birch

Nerthus can be invoked for:
Motherhood, Childbirth, Fertility, Care, Abundance, Honours, Riches, Wellbeing, Strength, Confidence, Speculative pursuits.

Ing (Ingui Fréa)

The God Ing is the brother to Freya and said to be the father of the present line of kings & Queens from notably England and Sweden. A God of peace and fertility for crops, cattle and humankind his Priesthood was noted by Tacitus to wear the garb of females sounding small bells and clapping whilst presiding over their religious ceremonies. Connected to Elves, Ingui Fréa whose symbol is the Boar (Protection) also served at least sometimes as a God of defensive War. We can equate these two attributes in as much as it would have been impractical to be a defensive deity as this would require the services of most of the men marching off to battle thus making the fertility of the fields none existent. So a "defensive War God" connects perfectly with the concept of his fertility.

An effigy of Ingui Fréa like the Goddess Nerthus was paraded throughout the many villages of Anglo Saxon England. It stood upright secured upon a wagon or wain but unlike the Mother Goddess he was not veiled but "shown off" in all his finery surrounded by a large following of his devoted Priesthood. Both Freya and Ing are indeed sister and brother share the Boar as their symbol or "Totem Animal" with mythological sources pointing to a very special boar being made by dwarves named 'Golden Bristles' that became a significant magical icon on which oaths would later be sworn by English Kings at Yule.

The God Ing can be invoked for:

Growth, Seductive elements, Fertility, Potential, Self awareness, Time, The curing of Impotence and all issues of Sexuality.

Rune: ᛝ

Tree: Hazel/Fruit trees.

Hel (Goddess of Death)

Odin sent the Goddess Hel to rule over the domain of the dead when he cast out herself and her two brothers for their malice and mayhem ravaged upon the worlds.

Jormungand 1st brother and known as the world snake, was cast into the deepest depths of the ocean whilst the other brother Fenris the wolf was held by a huge chain in order to hold him fast to prevent his escape.

Hel is seen as the embodiment of death, whilst Jormungand became the embodiment of pain leaving the fearsome Fenris to embody the essence of sin, all three having one of the most dubious of parents Loki who himself maybe the altar ego of the god Odin.

The world of this Goddess is one of impenetrable darkness and unbearable cold. The rivers of this dark, dark place twist and writhe with undercurrents of concealed sharpened blades that only serve to add their menace to its most turbulent of waters. Interestingly enough the bed that Hel lays upon is known as, Sorrow and her knife is known as greed both fitting attributes of a Goddess who presides over those who have come to her through sickness, old age and murder. It is said that the gaping corpse-like jaws of Hel have never uttered the words that would ever permit her guests to leave that terrifying realm of doom, so no escape is at all possible once anyone has arrived at her door.

This Goddess of death however does not fetch the souls of her charges but awaits their arrival in her home called Nifolham where her serpents are said to spit scalding venom upon the bodies of the wicked.

Invoking Hel is ill advised but if one did consider such a task then all one needs to do to halt the malicious and wicked souls that plague our lives is to simply say, three times over "Go to Hel" and soon enough they may embark upon a road to wrack and ruin.

NB: It is also important to note that many of the gods used by the burgeoning practitioners of Anglo Saxon Witchcraft were a cross over between Norse/Viking and Saxon deity.

Seaxneat (God Ancestor of the English Saxons)

Founder of the Saxons the god Seaxneat/Saxnot is the champion god of the blade and ancestor god to the Kings of Essex. Seaxneat was eventually denounced by the Saxons in favour of the Christian god and alas little knowledge remains of this important link to our past and his attributes. He is often compared to other Saxon gods and although we know that the word Seax means Blade, the word neat, is offered as Animal/Beast/Ox it could also be said that this mysterious figure of the English could well be the original horned one of legend?

Other beings

Our Anglo Saxon Witch forbears were never ever quite so alone as you may think? For as the old texts state there were many other entities that shared the lives of the Lybléc and indeed all of humankind way back in the mists of time. These "other beings" or léasbréda (Sometime tricksters and deceit weavers) were known to transcend the 9 worlds of existence with sometimes devastating effect, so much so that is was advisable that one should be on one's guard at all times in order to overt the sometimes-evil intent and malicious spreading of disease/bad luck by these unwanted entities. Although it can be noted that all these supernatural entities were not "So bad" all of the time, it is interesting to note just how many of these beings, are still perceived to be around today, and are still firmly embedded in our psyche and English language.

Let's take a look at some of them.

aelf	Elf
deofol	Demon
draca	Dragon
dweorg	Dwarf
fægerfolc	Beautiful people/fairy folk
fæcce - fetch	Guardian
Fifel - grendel	Sea monster - Monster
gást	Spirit/Ghost
Ent - Eotnas	Giants
pucel	Goblin
Scucca - Shuck	Demon Dog
wight	Land Spirit/House Spirit

Elves
The Black Elves of Loki are creatures akin to Dwarfs/ Dwarves and will work magic against humans as can be noted in references such as that of the Water elf charm (For sudden pain) and their ability to harm and debilitate humans at will. White Elves/High Elves are beings of elegance, light and beauty. Having no shadows, they will assist those fighting the forces of Loki and his black Elven hoard but are never to be crossed, as all manner of bad luck shall follow.

Deofol
Even today, we cannot escape from the notion of Devils and Demons. They are part and parcel of the human race and have plagued us ever since the dawn of creation. Although the Christian Devil was primarily put there to "Scare you into submission" so that the masses could be "Clergy controlled", the demons of the Anglo Saxons, were closely linked to death and the world of the Goddess Hel. Our devils were seen as having more to do with our own earthly actions and the consequences thereof in the after life æfterlif and had little to do with anything associated with priestly control and subservience to the church.

Draca
The dragon is mentioned in *Beowulf.* It guards a great treasure but is defeated by the mortally wounded Beowulf. King Vortigern was advised to sprinkle the blood of a fatherless child onto the foundations of a stronghold he would build against the settling Anglo Saxons. His Magicians bade him do this as it was said that beneath their feet lived two dragons, one representing the Britons and red in colour and the other white that represented the oncoming Saxons. Needless to say his magic failed and when the dragons were roused the White Saxon Dragon defeated the red dragon and in so doing, symbolised a new era and the rise of the English as a nation.

Dweorg

The word for dwarf/dweorg has a strange connection with the causing of such ailments as fits fevers and uncontrollable trembling, but one thing is for sure their mastery of metalwork is second to none. It was the dwarfs that fashioned Mjöllnir the hammer of THOR.

F gerfolc

The chain that held Fenris/Fenrir the wolf was made by the wee folk and called Gleipnir. It was extremely light but strong in its construction, and was made of such things as "the noise from the footsteps of a cat" and "The roots of stones" and even fugolspit the saliva of birds.

Fetch

A guardian spirit or totem animal that represents our disposition within the realms of our everyday and spiritual lives. This other world "Familiar" can pass on our "Good luck" or good spiritual energy to us, and serves as a "Watcher" who notes our bad deeds which in turn corresponds to how much good energy we may receive. The origins of the fabled Witches Black Cat.

Fífel - Grendel

From manuscripts found by Sir Robert Cotton in 1731, we have the now legendary Beowulf. This tale tells of Grendel the hellish monster grim, greedy, brutal and cruel, which prowled the misty moors as a dark deathly shadow. But even so Heathens made sacrifice to the one they call the "The soul destroyer" as they held rites in their "Pagan tabernacles" for help in their direst distress.

Gást

In some way or another all of the above can be termed as Ghosts. From the Land Wight's, to house spirits all are part and parcel of the nine worlds of existence. A glimpse of such ghosts can be caught of out of the corner of your eye whilst not concentrating but as suddenly as they are seen they disappear when you intentionally look directly at them. Our ancestors are also seen as ghosts as they call to us from the realms of the dead, but can manifest into our world, breaching the boundaries of our consciousness in exceptional circumstances.

Ent

The eotnas are giants who are closely linked with the gods. It is said that they are of varying sizes but for the most part they are not malevolent beings, but powerful and very wise.

Puccel

The Christians termed Puck, the Devil himself? An evil creature whose mischievous acts of malice and mayhem closely linked to that of a Poltergeist. To ward off his "Meddling" offerings of Milk & Honey were sometimes left out in the hope that this would "Calm the Puck".

Scucca

Ghostly black dogs also known as a Shuck, it roams the moors and grave yards with its red glowing eyes, sometimes with two heads or no head at all, these black messengers of doom can vanish at will. These terrible hounds have been seen throughout the length and breadth of the British Isles for hundreds of years, and to witness one of these "Witch hounds" has always been equated with a sense of foreboding as they are messengers of death for either the person who spied them, or their loved ones.

Wights

Tree spirits, land spirits, house spirits and even the ancestors are all known as Wight's. Although normally, these entities dwell in the realms outside our everyday perceptions, they "Can" be seen and appeased through dream-states, magic or through trance work. It is said that the very young and those adults who retain a true sense of wonder are especially prone to see them, as are our pet dogs and those who are suffering from illness. Land Wight's and House Wight's are thought to help control the wellbeing, safety and fertility of the countryside and of our homes. These spirits should be given regular offerings of bread & honey on or around the main festivals. The spiritual sustenance should be placed upon a stone in a secluded spot and left until the next time.

When doing the same for the house Wight, the offerings should be placed at the highest part of the dwelling i.e.; in the loft or attic to insure the cooperation and benevolence of the spirit in question.

Lyblác elements

Some may consider that the elements or "quarters" should not be associated with or are not in line with northern or Anglo Saxon thinking? This is simply wrong, if you consider the four dwarves of Northern creation mythology i.e.: Nordri (North) Sudri (South) Austri (East) Vestri (West) that held up the four corners of the sky made from the Ymir`s skull. It is not difficult to make the connection that north, south, east and west are named after these legendary dwarves, so why not use them in veneration and respect helping us to support and promote our own craft and skills.

Below goes some way to showing how we of the Lyblác venerate and celebrate the quarters of Anglo Saxon Witchcraft. The specific rune can be traced in the air at the appropriate direction using a sword or blade of some kind.

*NB: At the beginning there was ice and the ice was all and could not be tamed. Then fire came into existence, becoming the source of change/transformation the breath of the gods carried this new force to the ice and ice smelted, creating the flowing waters of life. It flowed over the earth giving nourishment and creation. A never ending cycle.

North

(Ice)

ᛁ

A.S.
Welga norðlic frætwa
Ealdfæder
Izas rún geðn éadig

Hail northern Jewels
Ancient fathers
Ice rune, blessed of courage

*[PP]
well-ga north-lik fray`t-wah

ey-ald fay-der

ee-sass roo-n

ge-thin ay-dig

The Izas rune represents: The North. Ice. Tapping inner resources. Self consciousness. Creation. Enlightenment. Guidance. Force. Ice can halt water and crush stone.

South

(Fíre)

ᛋ

A.S.
"Welga brynebeorg
Ælanland
Sigil rún" spéd éadig

Hail burning mountain
scorched land
Sun rune, blessed of success

[PP]

Well-ga brin-a-borg

Ale-an land

Sigil roo-n

Spe-yd ay-dig

The Sigil rune represents: The South. Fire. The Fire mountains. Movement. Primeval beginnings. Protection. Opposite of Ice. Purpose. The higher self. Success. The will. The Forge, Humankind.

East

(Aír)

ᛖ

A.S.
"Welga eastwind
Ferhðland
***Ehwaz rún"* godes éadig**

Hail eastwind
Realm of the mind
Horse rune, blessed of Gods

*[PP]

Well-ga ay-st wind

Fair-th land

Eh-wass roo-n

God-es ay-dig

The Ehwaz rune represents: The East, Air, Working together. Harmony. Acceptance. Loyalty. Trust. Partnership. Breath of the gods. The sky mare. Swift action.

West

(Water)

ᛚ

A.S.
Welga nâ bridel
gæbrecwaðum
Laguz rún" inbryrdnes éadig

Hail no bridal
crashing wave
water rune, blessed of inspiration

*[PP]

Well-ga nay-breed-al

Gah-brek wah-thum

Laa-gus roo-n

In-beerd-nes ay-dig

The Laguz rune represents: The West. Water. Life. Force. Growth. Potential. Ebb & Flow. .Journeys. Stamina. Hope. The unknown. The sea mare "No Bridal".

Earth

(Erce)

ᚷ

A.S.
Welga eorthan mòdor
Nerthus
Gyfu rún fyllu éadig

Hail earth mother
Erca
gift rune, blessed of abundance

*[PP]
Well-ga earth-an mor-dor

Er-ka

Gif-oo roo-n

Fill-oo aydig

The Gifu rune represents: Earth. The Mother. Gifts. Hospitality. Wishes granted. Abundance. Honour. Nature & Nurture. The female. Offspring.

[Make the sign of each rune in the air with the sword as you recite the above.]

Now say:

"þes godes hearg ond ic heora cynn   weard --- wacian--- warian --- friðian"

"This, gods temple and I there kin. Ward, Watch, Warn and give peace"

PHO

Thes god-es her-g
Ond itch hear kin
Where-d
Watch-ian
Warr-rian
Frith-ian

A New Name

In many cultures around the world as a person becomes more attuned and knowledgeable in the ways of his/her religion, and wishes to take up a more committed or Priestly position within their chosen path the consensus is, that they begin to seek a new and for the most part more appropriate working or magical title. This is of special significance, especially in this bustling "Gotta get there fast" society that we all live in to day. We need to be able to differentiate between our every-day 9 to 5 existences as Jon/Jane Doe living in this modern frantic dog-eat-dog world from our religious, more feeling and spiritual/magical selves, dedicated to our Gods, our traditions and the well being of those around us

Titles & Names

The chosen name and of course subsequent titles should not be too elaborate and only used in your religious life. I would think it quite impractical if you did not do this. Imagine a receptionist calling out something like, 'Wulfeage, Seax Gesith, High Priest and ealdormann of the Lyblác High Witan' whilst sitting in a full Dentist waiting room! Although it may well clear the seats we can all do without the bigotry of those who are not so understanding of who we are or what we do as Priests or Priestesses of Anglo Saxon Witchcraft. So of course we should be aware that it is better to separate our two personas especially when dealing with none Pagans and refrain from giving ourselves such grandiose titles. So Wulfeage, Priest of Lyblác becomes more than sufficient.

Naming Rite

[Firstly you will have to choose your new religious name/title.]

[Perform the affirmation of the hearth]

[On the Altar should be your "Galdra bòc" (Book of Shadows) and something to write with.]

[You should go "Skyclad" having bathed and removed all jewellery.]

[The declaring of the temple should be performed.]

Standing before the Altar in the ᛉ position say:

"Here do I stand before the mighty ones, naked and unadorned
My plea is for kinship of the Gods and of the Lyblác
and wish it known that I have taken a new name".

Taking up the salted water sprinkle some on top of your head say:

"Blessed is this sacred water and blessed are the Gods
Father, Mother of all life hear me now
This water anoints me. My name is ....
Let this be a worthy name for a Priest / Priestess of your love".

Putting down the water, open your Galdra bòc and write your name, after which return to the Algiz position and say:

"Woden, Frigg: I place my name in your safekeeping
let this name be honourable
let this name be true
Let it be known by rock & sky by river and by the wind

by tree and by all that dwell upon, in, and over the Earth
As ...... Name... Priest / Priestess of the Gods

So mote this be.

Stand for a while with your eyes closed, seeing with your mind's eye a white light covering your body. Suddenly the light will cease and your eyes will open.

[Perform the sealing of the hearth].

[Here are some Anglo-Saxon names you may wish to adopt, but you should always make sure that the name that is chosen reflects your personality or standing. You may even ask the gods themselves to reveal your new name if you so desire!

In my particular case although my real name is Sean Percival it has been said on many occasions that because of my pale green eyes that they resemble those of a Wolf, hence the Anglo Saxon name that I have adopted "Wulfeage - Wolf's eyes"]

M...Ingwulf	Ing`s Wolf
M...Wulfeage	Wolf Eyes
F....Gydenár	Goddess Messenger
F... Hræfnfeax	Raven Hair
M...Fréomæg	Free Kinsman
M...Ordfruma	Warrior/Vanguard
F....Mægwyn	Delightful Maiden
F....Bearumódor	Grove Mother
M ...Lárlist	Skilled of Lore
M...Hræfen	Raven

F....Fréodóhtor Freeborn daughter
F....Aelfwynn Joy of the Elves

Working out one's name can be very gratifying, full of added meaning with a great connection to our Anglo-Saxon past.

swið	Strong
Rædbora	Advisor
Gast	Spirit
Eolhsand	Amber
Déor	Animal
Bera	Bear
Léoma	Beauty
Hold	Faithful
Móna	Moon
Lytel	Little
Stán	Stone
Wulf	Wolf
Weorð	Worthy
Fugol	Bird
éadig	Blessed
Beald	Bold
Bár	Boar
Swan	Swan
Cráwe	Crow
Ellen	Bravado
Sunne	Sun
Wilde	Wild
Đeoden	Chief
Mergen	Morning
Est	Favour/Grace
Fréo	Free
ár	Messenger
Mægen	Might
Heort	Stag
Steda	Stallion

All of the above A. S. words can be found in Stephen Pollington`s book "*Wordcraft*" New English to Old English Dictionary and Thesaurus.

Lyblaeca: Priest of the gods/Witch/Sorcerer. One proficient in the art of magic.

Lybbestre: Priestess of the gods/Witch/Sorceress. One proficient in the art of magic.

Altar & Dress

The Lyblác Altar differs from that of other Pagan traditions in as much as although it can stand within a sacred circle, its design and "Dressings" are personal to the Lyblaeca/Lybbestre themselves. There should however be representations and offerings that pertain to the kind of ritual you will be perform-ing, and of course the season of the year at which you find yourselves. There are no hard and fast rules as to what Godly or elemental representations you may place upon your Altar. For some, a skull, bones or even just a black disc on which a black candle is placed can symbolise the "Unknown" there are many alternatives that can be used; which all depend on the creativity and personality of the individual when working as a Lyblác Witch.

The Altar itself can be placed anywhere within the circle, again pertaining to the sort of ritual you will be undertaking at the time, offerings or symbols can be placed at the five elemental points as well as upon the Altar.

In the North: for all things to do with protection, consecration, cohesiveness. Ice strength.

In the East: For communications, the mind, light and the intellect. Air breath of the gods.

In the South: For expansion and energy and fire

In the West: For fluidity and stillness. For the natural flow and the depths of un-manifested energy. Water. The Ocean.

Hearth, Earth: For abundance and all potential. For nature and nurture. The ancestors. Nerthus, the mother of all life.

Dress

Again unlike modern Wiccans those of the Lyblác did not wear multicoloured velvet robes emblazoned with the odd penta-gram or two. They wore the same or very similar cloths as every one else of that time, only being distinguished as a Lyblác Witch by their elaborate staff, the key and of course word of mouth. I myself do wear a black robe and tabard (old habits die hard) with a plaited red, black and white cord. The black and white cords are there to represent light & dark, day & night, male & female, i.e. the balance of all things. And the red is for the blood of humankind and of the gods that weave their way through everything. The only advice is to wear what you think appropriate but a black tabard over the top with a coven or runic symbol on the chest can look most effective!

The Circle

Way back in the mists of time as our ancestors sat around their encampment fires, it was of no doubt, that the welcoming heat, light and sound of the flames not only served to keep them warm and alive, but also acted to ward off ferocious and hungry animals. It is easy to make the connection that from this outer circle of light produced by the campfire, that it was deemed the edge of magical & physical protection. As fire, it was given to humankind by the Gods, the shape and form of its protective and defensive boundary became more and more entwined into the symbolism and minds of the people. The circle itself would take on magical properties, and was used as the basic shape in the construction of houses, and even the warrior's shield became circular in design and was seen as having a magical connection encompassing all the physical and godly attributes that would aid its owner.

The number 3 also became of great significance to the Anglo Saxon Lyblác of England. Anything vaguely magical would have had to be in multiples of 3. The circle we use today and made up of eight stones with a central hearth (making 9) is a physical representation of the protection of Brosingamene the necklace belonging to the Goddess Freya.

This stone circle is this shape and form because the Lyblác Wicca, manifest unshaped energy/power within, so that it can be directed and projected using the astral body and the gods (with the help of the staff) to spiritually travel into the realms of the nine worlds.

Items adorning the Altar should include:

An Altar cloth

A Drinking horn

A bowl

Deity representations

Candles

Incense

[The tale of Freya & Brosingamene can be found on page 19 of
The Tree.
The Complete Book of Saxon Witchcraft. Raymond Buckland
Also page 18 of Buckland's book of Saxon Witchcraft]

Consecration

For thousands of years humankind has practised the art of "dedicating" or the "making holy" of certain ritual objects, people and places as part of our religious and spiritual heritage. The act of consecration or sacrifice has a well-worn and enduring path, it cleanses and strips away all negativity giving direction and makes the object of dedication pure and free from all influences that have connected with it in its past. It is interesting to note that I have used the word "sacrifice" which many have steered clear of because of its supposed nature, making it loaded with connotations of blood and death. In its original form (Anglo-Saxon not Christian); it is not necessarily connected with the killing of animals or people! The word as it originally was, and is in reality still means "To make holy" not as some Churchmen would have us believe "a means of gaining sadistic pleasure from putting some poor soul to their deaths in a diabolic rite full of sex and abomination". Thankfully, the tide has turned and people are questioning some of the so-called old truths and taking back their heritage.

The act of consecration or sacrifice is to dedicate whatever ritual object, tool or place to a higher level of consciousness and purpose. That something, someone, or somewhere can become a forceful catalyst that in turn can cause important and magical "things" to happen, a holy unity between source, purpose, man and the Gods. It is as much a part of the magical and religious connective to day as it ever was, and from the depths of our past, it is still an integral part of our ever-evolving Pagan lives.

[The following Hammer Rune consecration rite can be adapted to any ritual item the length between the runes just being greater or smaller so the item can be placed upon them:]

Consecration rite

(Hammer rite for magical tools)

[The Affirmation of the hearth is performed.]

Take the elemental rune staves placing them in the hammer positions half their length into the earth:

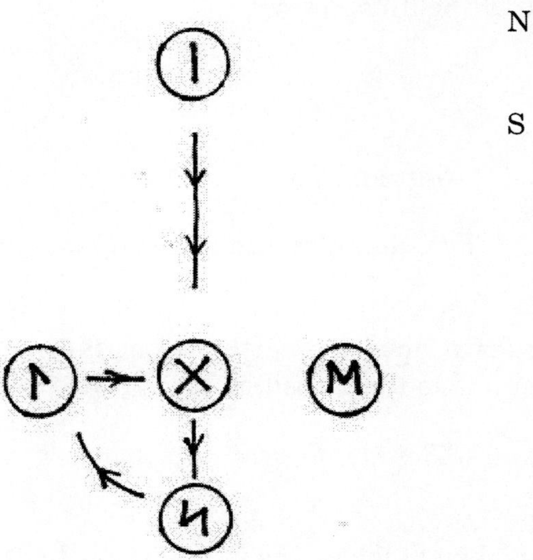

Place the item to be consecrated on top of the rune staves in the hammer formation. Stand at the southern end of the hammer in the ᛉ position.

Facing Northward Say:

*"Ancestors, here is the (sword, Seax, staff) of ....name....
forged of earth and fire, from the magic of the void
Fashioned of will and Gods embrace
Long may it serve me blessed of purpose"*

Turn to the East and say:

"Let the winds behold the singing of the blade".

Turn to the South and say:

"Show now forces of fire and serpents bite"

Turn to the West and say:

"Be fluid unleashed of no bridal quenched"

Laying down upon the earth still at the southern tip of the hammer and in the ᛉ position say:

"Born of the belly and victory blessed"

Now stand and take up the sword/blade/staff pointing it to the North, now turn the tool flat at arms length and draw a circle in the air around you with the tool. Once this is done point the tool straight up into the air hold it there for a short while then swinging the it downwards to the earth then back up to the sky saying as you do so:

Of highest mountains and waters deep
....Say aloud the name of the tool....
Thunor, Ward, Watch
Protect and Keep.

Taking the sword/blade/staff and holding it to your mouth say gently:

***** *àn galdor geðrùen*
*þunor halig gifu***

The tool is now consecrated and dedicated to serve you. Let none other than direct kin ever handle the tool.

(* A charm forged, Thunor blessed gift.)

Affirmation of the Hearth

As you may already know from reading *The Tree* by Raymond Buckland an integral part of the Seax tradition is the Erecting or Declaring of the Temple. The Temple is declared firstly; to show respect for the Gods but also to honour that sacred place in which you have chosen to hold your rites, recognising its sacredness and Godly essence.

In Lybläc Anglo Saxon Witchcraft the consecration of this sacred place is termed: The Affirmation of the Hearth and is performed at the start of every rite.

The Lybläc Witch: *Lyblaeca (m) and Lybbestre (f) should normally mark out the Hearth/circle with his/her staff. The Priest or Priestess should already have prepared the Altar and if with others should act as a watch-person to oversee the assembling worshippers before, they enter the declared sacred space. Either in a group or alone the affirmation of the Hearth should be performed in the same way and is as follows:

Affirmation of the Hearth

[After carefully choosing your site place on your Altar some wine, mead or ale or none alcoholic beverage if you prefer. A small drinking horn or chalice, incense and 3 candles Red, White & Black. Some representation of the God & Goddess. Salt, Water, bread and a sprig of evergreen. All of this being particular to the Lyblaeca/Lybbestre themselves]

Lyblaeca / Lybbestre

Lights the Altar candles and then takes the white candle and proceeds to light the perimeter candles. Then taking up his/her Staff, Spear or Seax marks out the circle saying:

"Here do I affirm this Hearth
In peace and with Love do I honour it
May the mighty Thunor hallow and make all sacred
So that in all ways and in all things
Shall the Mother's embrace be upon me / us
Swá willan ic / wê"

Stand before the Altar:

Taking up the Salt holding it in both hands raised above your head saying:

"This Salt is pure. Life is of this Salt!
And in its purity shall it purify my life
Blessed shall it be and in turn all my / our rites
In honour of the Mother and Father
Woden and Frigg."

*Lyblaeca (m) and Lybbestre (f) Priest/Priestess.

Swá willan ic / wê – So wish I / We.

Tipping a small portion of the Salt into the water stirring it with a piece of the evergreen say:

"This blessed Salt shall hold all fast
and cleansed now is this water.
In all my / our rites shall purity reign

That together in the service of my / our Gods
They shall banish aught that would do harm."

Holding the bowl of sacred liquid in one hand and the evergreen in the other walk deosil around the circle dipping the sprig and sprinkling and purifying the Hearth saying:

"This is a sacred place, a righteous testimony."

[Place the bowl back upon the Altar]

Taking up the incense "cense" the area in the same way repeating the above line.

Now stand before the Altar dipping your fingers in the salted water. Make the mark of a circle on your chest then raising both arms *

Turn and face South reciting the Lyblác call:

The Lyblác Call

Hail to the God and Goddess
Our Lord and our Lady.
Hail to the might of Woden
Hail to Erce`s bounty.
Hail to you witches all
And kin to this company.
In Love.
In Life.
In Peace.
In Light.
In Truth.

In Harmony.
So shall this be now and evermore.

* The arms of the Lyblaeca / Lybbestre should be now raised in a ᛉ position facing the centre.

Lybaeca/Lybbestre says:

The Gods welcome all with Love in their hearts to this hearth
The sky father and earth mother
Shall watch and keep us all in their embrace
Peace and love now reign
And let none ever leave us without just cause.

Take up your blade (Seax in Anglo-Saxon) place a kiss on the metal. Now with your other hand take up the Blowing Horn. Point the blade, arm out stretched in the direction of the element. Sound the Horn three times then lowering the Horn say the following in a clear and forceful manner:

[The Anglo Saxon Lyblác elements can be used in place of the English version stated also below. Recite the verse for the Lyblác elements North, South, East, West, and then Earth.]

Facing the Altar say:

"First was everything ice, dark and frozen without life
I acknowledge the great powers of the North and of Ice
I bid thee......Welga ond wilcume!"

"Welga norðlic frætwa
Ealdfæder
Izas rùn"geðyn éadig"

Turn to the South:

"*Then came* fire. Light and heat were born
I acknowledge the great powers of the South and of Fire
I bid thee...... Welga ond *wilcume!*"

"Welga brynebeorg
Ælanland
Sigil rùn " spéd éadig"

Now turn East:

"Then came the breath of the gods that blew the heat of the
Fire Mountains
I acknowledge the great powers of the East and of Air
I bid thee...... Welga ond wilcume!"

"Welga eastwind
Ferhðland
Ehwaz rùn "godes éadig"

Turn to the West:

"The ice melted and the scorched earth was healed
I acknowledge the great powers of the East and of Air
I bid thee...... Welga ond wilcume!"

"Welga nâ bridel
Gæbrecwaðum
Laguz rùn "inbryrdnes éadig"

Now stand midway between the north of the circle and the centre of the Hearth. Kneel down facing the centre. Point the blade earthwards blow 3 times on the horn, look down and in a softer voice say:

"The waters flowed upon the earth giving life and nourishment
and the realm of humankind was born.
*I acknowledge thee, all Mother, the great powers of the Erce**

and of the Earth
I bid thee...... Welga ond wilcume!

"Welga eorthan mòdor
Erca
Gyfu rùn "fyllu éadig"

Stand up and turn back towards the Altar, arms raised in the Algiz position and say:

"Here do I now invite the Gods Woden and Frigg / Frigga;
You who are husband and wife and kin to us all
Guide me / us and protect me / us in my / our rites
in all things and in all ways
now and for evermore."

So Shall This Be.

"þes godes hearg ond ic heora cynn weard --- wacian--- warian --- friðian"

"This, gods temple and I there kin. Ward, Watch, Warn and give peace"

Turn again to the South holding your blade (Seax) in one hand and the Drinking-Horn in the other. Place a kiss upon the metal of the blade then hold it in front of you outstretched toasting the Gods with a loud:

"To Woden and to Frigg / Frigga".

Now take a drink from the horn after which you should spill a small amount upon the ground and say:

"For the Mother"

Place the items back on the Altar turn back to the centre of the circle and say out loud:

"THIS TEMPLE STANDS"

gestanden is ðæt hearg

NB: If others are present then the acting Priest/Priestess should mark them on entry to the Hearth/Temple with the sign of the circle and a place a kiss upon the left cheek. This is done only when the Hearth has been affirmed. The Priest or Priestess can affirm the Hearth either together or alone.

If you are just a couple alone then you should mark each other and kiss.

* Erca is the ancient Anglo Saxon name for mother Earth (Nerthus) the 'c' is pronounced as a "K". *Swá willan ic / wê* equates to (So wish I/Us). If enough other celebrants are present then they should recite the A.S greeting on the four quarters with the Lyblaeca / Lybbestre performing the fifth element of mother earth.

* The words "*Welga on wilcume*" mean hail and welcome and are self-evident. It can also be noted from the above that our Witch ancestors recognised as many as 5 elements, but sometimes as few as 2.

* Although Lybĺác is mainly a solitary tradition when the Lyblaeca / Lybbestre calls the Gods to "welcome all with Love in their hearts to this Temple" he/she does so because no matter where in the world we find ourselves we are together in spirit as practitioners of the Lybĺác tradition.

Ale & Bread

(Ealu ond hláf)

An integral part of any ceremony is the winding up of events. In order for the celebrants to gel and become a "family" in and out of their ceremonial workings, the winding down and bonding of the kinship should take place. It is also important for Solitary Lyblác Witches to feel that they are not alone at this time and should celebrate the Ale and bread part of the proceedings as being part and parcel of the greater Lyblác craft and community.

All assembled should have taken a gift of Bread along to the proceedings along with their own drinking horn or suitable vessel together with some Ale or Mead.

Lyblaeca or Lybbestre should have the bread, salt and ale/mead on the altar. After filling the drinking horn or chalice they should take up the seax and turn to the centre of the circle.

Standing once again the ᛉ position bidding all assembled to take up their own blades and point towards the centre of the hearth.

Lyblaeca/Lybbestre then says:

God and Goddess
Mother and Father
Here do I / we stand your kin

Turning back to the altar the Lybaeca/Lybbestre picks up the drinking horn or chalice and turning back to the circle tips some of the beverage onto the earth saying:

To Woden and to Frigg
And to the mother

Lyblaeca/Lybbestre then takes a sip for themselves and raises the drinking vessel saying:

And to all Lybĺác
Who live and love in the sight of our Gods.

The libation is then passed around to all celebrants re-filling if need be. When all have taken a drink the drinking horn or chalice is then placed back upon the altar.

Now, the attention is directed towards the Ale/Bread. The Lybaeca/Lybbestre breaks the bread into bite-sized pieces and then takes a pinch of salt and sprinkles it over the cakes/ bread saying:

We give thanks to Erca
For the abundance that she bestows upon us
We now share in her delight
And nurture of her children
To give is to receive
To rejoice in that giving
Is the richness of the mother's love.

Now turning to the centre and taking a piece of bread the Lyblaeca/Lybbestre crumbles it onto the Earth saying:

Erca, Erca, Erca Earth Mother of humankind
Love and eternal thanks be upon you.

The bread is now passed around the other celebrants and in doing so the first line of the above should be recited by the acting High Lybaeca/Lybbestre to which the recipient of the food should answer:

Love and eternal thanks are upon her.

Now all can get their own food and beverages and sit and share what they have and discuss anything dear to their hearts.

Ealu is Anglo-Saxon for Ale and is pronounced "Eh-leh".
Hláf is A.S. for Bread
Cicel is A.S. for Cakes. "C" in old English is pronounced as a K.
Meadu is A.S. for Mead.
Sealt is A.S. for Salt.

Seal the Hearth

At the end of every rite the Hearth must be sealed. This is done to release all energies that have been built up during your rites and to release all parties from their attendance. The acting High Lyblaeca/ Lybbestre should stand and blow the horn. This should be the signal for all attending to take their blades and holding them with both hands clasped around the handle stand at the centre of the Hearth. All points should now face the centre downward toward the mother. The Lyblaeca/Lybbestre after placing the horn back on the altar joins them and says:

From near and from far we have journeyed here
In peace and in Love and kinship we have rejoiced
The bonds that we have felt shall never fail us
And our Gods ever present shall live in our hearts.

Woden, Frigg and all that favour
We thank you for your attendance
And as we part, your Love shall go with us
Hail and farewell to our Gods
Hail and farewell to all our brothers and sisters

All: *Hail and farewell.*

All present shall return to the edge of the circle and then each in turn approach the High Lyblaeca/Lybbestre kissing them on the cheek saying:

Hail and farewell sister / brother

A horn is blown at each of the five elements with the words "*Hail and farewell to the powers of* ...xxx......." starting at with Earth, then West, East, South, finishing in the North. The Lyblaeca/Lybbestre shall repeat it back if others are performing the elemental farewells and when the last celebrant has finished their recitation the Lyblaeca/Lybbestre shall say out loud:

This Hearth is sealed.

Lyblác Oath

The Oath of the Lyblác is taken when one feels ready to commit one's self to the way of the Anglo Saxon Witch. Sit quietly by yourself; light a white candle, whilst holding a large brass key. Play some soothing music and envisage yourself sitting by a large campfire. In your mind's eye also see those of your kin that have gone before. Feel the togetherness, feel the love and know that you are never alone. Now see the faces of your loved ones reflect the glow of the fire, food and drink are plentiful and suddenly you notice that the gods are sitting amongst you, your kin beckon you to come forward to stand before your gods, you willingly oblige and recite as you do:

Lords and Ladies, Gods and Goddesses
I encircle myself within this temple of your Love
May you know me now most deeply

Let the wisest of your words enlighten my heart
And may your love unfold the secrets of the ages
For here do I pledge my troth

I am of the sky and thunders roar
I am of the seas and the flowing ice
My eyes burn of the fire
Without which naught could be
I am kindred of the earth
And the Mothers embrace
My shield is yours as is my truth
My love is yours as is wise council

I shall aspire to utter your wisdom all of my days
And will honour and defend that which is Lyblác.

Show the key to all present. Squeeze it tightly as you say with all conviction:

This key is the tool that unlocks all truth
This key I shall wear as a symbol of my craft
And all those who walk this path of the Gods
I shall greet as brother and sister
and honour all in good faith

See the your gods surrounding you nod their heads in approval, then watch as the key you are holding glows, exuding a brilliant white light.

Now as Lyblaeca/Lybbestre you should write their name in runes upon a piece of bone. When this has been done, push the bone deep into the earth leaving it undisturbed never to be found by mortal souls. Now taking some Ale toast the gods and their power after which you should tip the rest over the spot of the buried bone.

NB: The inscribed name should be your new name. The inscription should be done with blood or red ochre. The oath can be undertaken indoors but obviously the burying of the bone is done in a secluded place and should be done within 24 hours.
The bone can be of any creature. The inscription can, if needs must, be done prior to the taking of the oath. The key should be worn on your right side around your waist. It should hang from a belt that has been plaited together from black, white and red cords.

Festivals

Yule

Geol. Twelfth Night.
(21st/22nd Dec - 1st/2nd Jan.)

Yule is twelve days of celebration starting at Yule Tide on the 21st/22nd of December and finishing on the 1st/2nd of January. Although the 21st/22nd is marked as the start of Yule where decorations are placed within the house and hearth it is not until the 12th night on the 1st/2nd of January that the actual "Yule" ritual should take place. This Geol celebration is for our Lord Woden, to send him strength and courage in the midst of his journey through this dark time. Also for continued health, wealth and happiness of our kindred until the cold and lifeless veil of winter has lifted.

Before the onset of evening on the 1st/2nd of January, all Yule decorations should be removed from the house and hearth and a Wassail bowl should be washed and dried and placed upon a bed of evergreen. A Yule cake known as the Twelfth Cake should have been baked that day to be offered to any celebrants later during the ritual. You can bake a smaller version of the cake if you are celebrating alone.

Our Lybläc brothers and sisters practice the custom known as "Wassailing" and together with their family and friends circle the hearth fire toasting each other's health, wealth and happiness whilst passing around and drinking from the Wassail Bowl.

The Hearth is affirmed (in a garden or secluded spot) and two white candles placed upon the altar with a third red candle placed in-between. In front of the candles should stand the Wassail Bowl resting on a bed of evergreen. To one side there should be 12 small white "Tea Light" type candles in suitable glass containers (for placing around the circle) and on the other side should sit the cake.

Standing before the altar the Lyblaeca /Lybbestre says:

The winter haunts us
Sadness reigns, as the light has grown dim
But there is one of our kin that needs our strength
And with our love we send it.

Lyblaeca/Lybbestre lights the left white candle saying:

This flame is to light your way Lord
A beacon in the long nights to show our / my love

Lyblaeca/Lybbestre lights the first of the twelve circle candles either placing it around the circle or giving to a celebrant to place in front of them within the circle. Then proceeds to light and place all of the other circle candles.

Now the attention is turned to the lighting of a fire at the centre of the Hearth after which the high Lyblaeca/Lybbestre steps to one side and standing in the ᛉ position says:

Lord Woden
Know that in this darkness of the harsh winter that we are with you
We have fashioned here hearth fire to light you on your way
And within these flames we bestow the gifts of strength, love and great courage

Know that the mothers blessed love is forever with you
And shall extol and glorify your return.

At this moment the white candle on the right side should be lit, wait a moment and then light the middle red candle. Now fill the Wassail bowl with beer, mead or sparkling wine. Turn to the centre of the hearth and say:

Brothers and sisters of the craft
The Gods and Goddesses protect and unite our paths
They bestow upon us blessings of health
blessings of wealth
and blessings of happiness
We are kept safe from the ravages of winter
to share the kinship, which is this family Lybléc
Hail to all the Gods and Goddesses
Hail to Erca dearest mother of humankind
And hail to us all Lybléc Wiccan.

Take a drink from the bowl and tip a drop onto the earth then pass it to the next celebrant saying: Health, Wealth and Happiness and in turn they should do the same. Break the cake and pass that around in the same way. Thereafter merriment and dancing shall follow until it is time to seal the Hearth.

NB: At this ritual, there is no need for the Cakes and Ale. If you are alone in your rites use a smaller bowl but know that you are celebrating with the whole of the Lybléc community.

Wassail also, *Ves heill*, Norse for "be in good health"

Wiccan is pronounced "Witch-ahn"
Winter Solstice
(1st day of Yule. December 21st)

Although today contemporary Pagan practice is to celebrate Yule for only one day on the 21st of December, our Anglo Saxon brothers and sisters the Lybléc celebrated the 12 days of Yule starting on the 21st/22nd of December ending with a Yule ritual on the 1st/2nd of January.

If you have ever wondered where the modern day practice of decorating the house at Christmas time comes from you only have to look at our Anglo Saxon heritage. The then Church needed to win over our Pagan forbears and so incorporated many of our indigenous Pagans practises into their own celebrations. However they did not realise that their intended action to destroy Pagan belief, actually served to preserve much of our Pagan religious heritage!

On the very first day of Yule homes are decorated with the finery of Holly, Ivy and Mistletoe. A Geol tree is erected and adorned with trinkets and coloured ribbons. (Recognise the connection with the Xmas tree?) An Oak log is set alight with the remnants of the former year's Yule Log (sacred to the God Thunar/Thunor) acting as counterpart to the fire of the Summer solstice.

Now in this day and age it may be a little difficult to light a Yule Log in a small municipal dwelling. Unfortunately there are some who do not have as much room or sufficient access as they would like, so it is quite permissible to alternatively use a Yule candle (Lit from the previous year's candle) and the appropriate blessings to celebrate the 12 days of Yule.

On the first day of Yule light the Yule Log/Candle whilst contemplating your journey over the past year. As you do so say

I kindle here this Yuletide flame
From the breath of summer

This life I charge
Steeped in joyous hearts and laughter
It holds fast the spark of Love
Which shall burn bright and true as the wheel turns again.

A.S.
Fram sumor æþm onælen ic Géol æled
þes lìf sculan of lustbære hleahtor steap
ond ðæt lufuspearc healden
bryne beorht ond sóðealswá ðæt hweohl bewendan

NB: All of the decorations and adornments should be kept for the whole twelve days of Yule. The candles/log/fire being re-lit every day

Lyblác New Year
(24th December)

If you have ever wondered where gift giving at Christmas time could come from then look no further than our Anglo-Saxon forbears. Traditionally the night of the 24th of December was the original "New Year" for the Witches over 1000 years ago. As the Christian church needed to "control" the Pagan population the birth of their Christian saviour Jesus was conveniently slotted into the indigenous Yuletide celebrations and became firmly fixed and is celebrated to this day.

The night of the New Year for our Lybláс brothers and sisters was a night of invitations & great feasting. Family and friends enjoyed themselves with merrymaking and "Gift Giving" (O.E. gift-giefan & nìwe-gèar-gift.) to strengthen the bonds of kinship and love.

The night is full of the "toasting" of family, friends and the Gods. It is quite easy to let yourself be inspired with your compliments that become friendly rivalry to see whose salutations are bolder and better and thus insuring a great time will be had by all.

Here are just a few you may use:

All hail to the God & Goddess
Mother and Father of all life
And hail to you all kith and kin
Health, wealth and a happy life.

Blessed, blessed am I with that which I love best
No fear, good beer and those I hold dear.

Be of good cheer.
The Gods give the gift of life
My husband / wife gave the gift of children
Mother Earth gives the gift of a full belly
And I am blessed with the gift of kinship.

My thanks to the Gods for a good life
My thanks for fertile seed
My thanks for the roundness of my form
And the greatest thanks is for my sharing with you all
Be of good cheer.

Mother's night

(The night of the 25th of December)

On this night all Goddesses are honoured especially the Goddess Nerthus (Erca) and of course the Goddess Freya. The rite itself, is an all night vigil celebrating the essence of the "Mothers" and solely celebrated by the womenfolk

At dusk the affirmation of the Hearth should be undertaken.

Lybbestre:

Here do I affirm this Hearth
In peace and in Love do I honour it
May the mother hallow and make all sacred
So that in all ways and all things
Shall the mothers embrace be upon me / us
So mote this be / Swa móten wé

She should now lay face down upon the earth saying:

This night of all our nights belongs to you mother.

You should now stand in the ᛉ position and say directly to the earth:

Erca.
Hail and welcome

Frigg.
Hail and welcome

Eostre.
Hail and welcome

Freya.
Hail and welcome

Hretha.
Hail and welcome

Nerthus.
Hail and welcome

I/we join this night in the holy sisterhood
An unbroken chain from mother to daughter
The union of blood
Since the dawn of humankind.

From this point on it is not known what the Lybláс sisterhood did in the rites. Whatever did happen was so secret that it was never written down but passed on from mother to daughter. At first light the Cakes and Ale should take place then the Hearth can be sealed.

Solmonath

(Imbolc. February eve)

This is a celebration of the God and Goddess as Mother Earth and Father Sky. The God has passed the hardest part of his journey through winters bitter grip and the Goddess rejoices and the earth starts to warm.

Ancient Roman texts call this the time "the month of cakes" and as the fields were ploughed and "planted cakes" together with poppet`s were placed therein to ensure the fertility of mother earth, Nerthus (Erca)

On the altar should be three white candles.
A poppet filled with straw.

A vessel that contains a mixture of milk & honey and number of cakes marked with these runes: -- ᚠ ᛒ and ᛋ

After the affirming of the Hearth is carried out the Lyblaeca/ Lybbestre cuts a piece of turf (approximately a square foot) from near the centre of the circle. The piece of turf should be taken and laid up side down, before the altar.

Lyblaeca/Lybbestre stands before the altar and lights the middle candle and says:

O father sky the light once dim is returning
The mothers embrace awaits our Lord
Know that our / my hearts / heart are / is with you
And that your path once so dark
Is passing into light.

Now light the second candle and say:

Know, mighty Lord the flame grows stronger
Lighting your way with our / my strength and our / my Love.

Now light the third candle and say:

This is the light of all life
That flame that is kept alive for your return

Lyblaeca/Lybbestre now takes up the milk & honey turning to the centre he/she says:

It is hard to weather the harsh times of winter
Spirits fade and strength wanes
Here do we give back to the Mother
From the gift we received is the gift we shall give
And nourished and nurtured the wheel once again turns.

The mixture is now tipped upon the earth side of the cut turf. The vessel is replaced upon the altar and the attention is turned to the straw filled poppet.

High Lyblaeca/Lybbestre takes up the poppet and stands above the hole made by the removal of the turf. Gripping the poppet in both hands and holding it above your head say:

Once one so dear lay upon her
Together in Love life was renewed
Remember our Lord
This poppet signals the bond and the return of seed
Fruit of his strength and his love is ever with the Mother
As she nurtures all in love eternal.

Place the poppet in the hole then the turf is retrieved and placed back from whence it came. Now kneel and place both hands upon the turf, say:

Together, once more
A divine promise of plenty
So mote this be.

Eft tógædre
Ùplìce fyllu gebéot
Swa mótan þes beón

Now follows the Cakes and Ale and as all eat a portion of the cake a small quantity is sprinkled upon the turf repeating the above three lines by each participant.

Hreðmonaþ

(Hrethmonath/Spring Equinox)

Hreth the warrior goddess is celebrated at the spring equinox, at this time we give thanks to her for allowing the cessation of ice upon the land that has plagued us through the harshness of winter and also for her help to facilitate us being victorious, surviving the battle over its bitter and biting cold. Fame and fortune can be won on this day if the right sacrifices are made and as with the ice and snow of winter that once covered and disguised the land, people should paint their faces and wear costumes which can be peeled away to reveal the reality that lies beneath.

Just as the heat of the sun melts away the snow and ice, so will the heat of the dance serve us to discard the layers of costume revealing the aching/surging sap of the flesh within. The quickening of the bud is the quickening of the lust for life. March being the last day of winter the rite of Hrethmonath is primarily to celebrate our victory over that season and the burgeoning springtime of bud and stem that will lead to the warmth of summer and the abundance of the coming harvest. The name Hrethe means victory, glory, triumph as well as being the title of a fierce and ruthless deity. So with the goddess's help we have all progressed another year, a favour won to the benefit of all.

Hrethmonath rite:

A fire is kindled in the hearth and all attending shall bring an offering to place in the fire. A bowl of seed shall be placed upon the Altar. A square of turf is opened.

Masks and costume are the order of the day with the overtone of "the brighter the better."

Masked and standing in the ᛉ position before the Altar the Lyblaeca / Lybbestre says:

This day is the day of Hreth
Victorious is she who has loosened the grasp of the harsh winter
We look now to the light, as the veil of darkness grows thin
The land once hidden is revealed in light
The warming of the seed quickens the bud
Passion is forged in the surging of the sap
And all shall live and love in the embrace of the mother
Rejoicing in the her beauty
Standing bold of purpose and firm in our triumph.

Taking the bowl of seeds the in the left hand the Lyblaeca / Lybbestre moves around the circle of participants and places a number of seeds into each person's left hand saying:

This is a time of birth
This is a time of burgeoning growth
A time to flourish
And a time to sow good seed

When they have finished passing out the seeds the Lyblaeca / Lybbestre returns to the Altar but stands facing the assembled folk and says:

To sacrifice to her is to give of your self

An gifu mæst seldsiene
A gift most rare

Ùre byre giefan
A gift of our time

Gecyðan for þu ùre lufu
Confirm we now our love for you

Sigedryten
Warrior goddess

Now shall all assembled one by one take their seeds throwing half of the measure into the fire. The other half should be held on to in order to plant at another location sometime, somewhere else that same day.

Once again you should eat, drink and be merry with lots of music and dancing and as the time moves on and the heat of the dance takes hold masks will fall, as what was always there shall be revealed.

Eostremonath

(Summer's arrival/Easter)

It is common knowledge that the Venerable Bede 679-735 wrote of this English goddess Ostara/Eostre in his work *De Temporum Ratione*, noting that the month Eostremonath was named after her and that she was venerated during the Start of Summer, which our forefathers celebrated in April. Eostre in the opinion of many is a spring/summer goddess and a goddess of rebirth; she is a celebration of life and nature taking on some of the attributes of the great earth goddess Nerthus. Many symbols surrounding the modern time of Easter can be directly attributed to the goddess Eostre/ Ostara. Eggs have come to symbolise this point in the festive calendar and are an obvious depiction of re-birth. Her timeless symbol the Hare has become the familiar "Chocolate Easter Bunny" but its origins are firmly rooted in the symbolism of potency with it being a virile exponent of force and fertility.

Hot cross buns with their obvious X rune markings are offered, eaten and placed upon the Altar at this time. The Buns themselves are said to be a representation of the four quarters of the moon and also the Sun Wheel. White, orange, red and yellow candles should also be lit and placed upon the Altar along with a hare's foot.

Lyblaeca/Lybbestre stands before the Altar and says:

A fire burns within our hearts
We look now to the eastern sky and welcome the dawn
Hail Eostre Bringer of summer
Hail Eostre

NB: All normal observances with regards to the affirmation and sealing the hearth should be undertaken.

Thrimilci

(Three milkings Beltane/May eve)

This time of abundance was known for the fact that cows could be milked three times in one day and was celebrated as a time of the richness of love, fire, light and of plenty. Our forefathers knew that through knowledge, hard work and devotion the gods would bestow upon them "Love & Light" and so they built large bonfires upon hilltops that lit the night skies as they danced, sang and courted new love infusing the festival with great passion, lust and desire. The sun's power ever increasing would soon enough be reaching its height at the forth coming solstice auguring in a time of ultimate potency and might. This time was also a time to share all that they had with their kith & kin knowing that, as they moved ever onward and further away from the darkness and the hardships of winter, together they could weather anything.

At Thrimilci we see a time of joyous song and fevered dance set to celebrate the falling away of shadow and the revelry in the lushness of life and the burgeoning fruit of Erce the earth mother. At this time the warming and lengthening days fill us with renewed energy and impetuses making us feel vibrant and alive! Thrimilci like the Celtic Beltane is a festival of radiance and the impelling force of nature that leads us all into the fevered celebration of Life, Light and Love with young and old alike chancing their arm in the hot and heated "open season" pertaining to affairs of the heart.

The rite

There shall be "flowers a plenty" decorating the Altar and indeed the homes of everyone. The name of Hearhden shall be used to drive away the spirits or bad Eotnas/Etins (Powerful beings/Giants) although it must be said that in Norse mythology although Hama/Heimdal was a good Etin, Loki certainly was not. It is and always was very prudent for all to keep his like at bay at this or any other time or else the king of mischief-makers could "run away" with our heart's desire.

A substantial fire shall be set and torches placed around the hearth. Standing before the Altar the Lyblaeca/Lybbestre calls to Hearhden by saying:

Hearhden mighty Smith, I / we call upon you this hour
Nine times I / we ask that you smite those that would steel my / our light
For you whose strength, sight and hearing are known throughout the worlds
Shall guard us and guide us as seekers of light.

Lyblaeca/Lybbestre faces the centre before he/she speaks and all attending turn to face outwards:

To those that would desire to darken our lives
This hearth fire shall show you the rage of Hearden`s heart
Quake should you who dare to stand before our door
Expect then no quarter, as none shall be given

[Throw a good-sized branch on the fire so as to make cinders and sparks fly into the air]

The might and strength of those that restored Freya`s heart and the light to all our lives
Shall halt the way of the uninvited, standing as a beacon to our love
And shall hold fast the dark desires of those that oppose the gods

All shall now turn back to face the centre, taking up the torches all together say:

mihtig heorte
ábréðan næfre
áwerian þæt léoht
ácléofan se mirce

Mighty heart
Never fail
Protect the light
Split the gloom

All should make great noise at this point waving the torches in the air, stamping feet etc.

As the jubilation dies down the Lyblaeca/Lybbestre shall say:

The light of love burns bright this night
Favour, favours the bold
And faint hearts shall never win loves promise
Let us live and let us love under the jewels of the heavens
So that the sweetest of all music shall flow as freely as milk
Let many granted wishes abound like stars in the sky
Leading captivated hearts to entwine in burning earnest
For as eyes meet eyes passion shall unfold

Tenderness shall seek from the seat of emotion
And thus as we touch, a delight in the beauty
So tender its gaze
So sweet its affection
A binding of souls
And a bonding of hearts
Of all pleasures compelling
The magnificent light of love

So shall this be

All:

So shall this be

[NB: This is now the time for boldness and passion as from the darkness of a lonely soul shall emanate the light of love to conquer the gloom. For those that are a little faint hearted concerning the opposite sex then the Lyblaeca/Lybbestre can act as matchmaker.]

Lítha

(Mid-Summer Solstice)

The two most important festivals of the Lyblác Witchcraft year are those of the summer solstice (Litha/Witches' night) and that of the winter solstice (Geol/Yule). Originally our ancestors were heedful of only two seasons, summer and winter. The mid-summer solstice and subsequent rite and festival celebrated the "summer season" the mid-winter solstice and subsequent rite and festival celebrated the "winter season". It must also be noted that both observances had specific "Moon guardians" namely Ærra Liða-Æftera Liða (Before and After Litha) and Ærra Geola-Æftera Geola (Before and After Yule) these were the full moons that waxed and waned before and after each festival.

Litha is reputed to mean the same as lithe namely: calm, gentle, gracious, meek, mild, serene, pleasant and sweet. This of course denotes the most agreeable and favourable type of weather that can accompany the time of "Flaming June" and the heady days when life is good and hearts warm, tender court feelings of contentment. The importance of fire at this time is quite obvious, our ancestors would make many fires and drive their cattle and livestock through the smoke in order to "Rid" them of pests and illness.

Litha rite:

The rite is performed at sunrise on the longest day of the year. Before hand a fire is kindled in the hearth earlier on the solstice eve with a vigil being held there so the fire can be kept burning and to "Watch" the fire through the night. Just before sunrise a ring of lit alternate yellow and red candles are placed around the circle where the celebrants shall gather. In between each alternate coloured candle shall be placed sprigs of evergreen and the whole area shall be besprinkled with sweet smelling flower petals. Amber and pine resin shall be placed upon the coals and mead shall flow a-plenty. All should have full drinking vessels/horns.

The Lyblaeca / Lybbestre stand before the rising sun and say:

Gladdened are we for this sun kissed morning
Love and life now reign in the halls of our hearts
Good company is abound and frith amongst us
Happiness and hope shall chase away all fear and sorrows
We share the love of the gods
And give of our love most freely
We salute the sacred union in freedom and faith
And rejoice in all our wellbeing hard won but never timeless
As we are strong in your service

The bold blessings of truth

Turning to all assembled the Lyblaeca / Lybbestre says:

Eat drink, and be merry
Let us toast the gods and the spirit of this new dawn
As we are touched by Sunna`s radiance
A true gift of the gods

Let us celebrate our togetherness
And the line unbroken

In gefĕrræden
ond in frið
in carléast
ond in geléaffulnes

All now drink from their drinking vessels/horns and say:

In friendship
And in frith
In freedom
And in faith

The Lyblaeca / Lybbestre now say:

Let us bring forth that which is to be cleansed
Let us cast away all doubt
As we offer that which shall be purged
Through the smoke of this sacred hearth fire
For the good and love of all.

As those assembled start to submit their offerings to and through the fire. [The mainstay of offerings will be "Wishes" written on parchment/paper]

The Lyblaeca / Lybbestre shall also say:

And to all lovers that would wish health, wealth and happiness
and everlasting love
I invite you now to leap this hearth

The lovers stand together hand in hand waiting until the Lyblaeca / Lybbestre deems it safe to leap. When it is safe the Lyblaeca / Lybbestre says:

May love's passion burn bright and as strong as this hearth fire
May the flames of love kindle strength in any wanting heart
Let the fires of excitement burn away all doubt
So that the ballad of loves dreams shall sound as sweet as any night singer

Love is the most precious of gifts
Granted by the gods.

Lyblaeca / Lybbestre gestures the lovers to leap. As the couples leap all present should cheer and say with loud voices:

Hail love's young dream
For they are truly blessed.

NB: At the closing of the rite, all those present shall hug and kiss each other and take pleasure in knowing the love, togetherness and loyalty of your kith and kin.

Lovers who "Leap the hearth" should hold each other's hand whilst leaping together. In their free/empty hand they shall hold a handful of flower petals and seeds which are released into the fire as they leap over it.

All manner of flowers and seeds are gathered throughout the day and are used to decorate everything from wells to homes. Various "Seeing" games are also played to catch a glimpse of any future lover. And a good party and get together should take place later that day, with the exchanging of small gifts such as mead/ale and tokens of love and friendship that shall keep the bonds strong.

Any "Night Singer" refers to the nightingale (nihtegala).

Haerfestmonath

(Haligmonath /Autumn Equinox)

The Christians changed the original name of this month/ festival (Haligmonath, Holy Month the time of devilish tribute) to Harvest Month (Haerfestmonath) in an attempt to make it sound much less Pagan, and at that time, the celebrations were directed to the great harvest Queen, Mother Nerthus. The Goddess Erce as she was also referred to was noted as a most bounteous deity and in her aspect as the "giver" just like the Norse goddess Gefjon she can be seen as "Mother Nature" and as with the symbol of earth (X) is represented by the Anglo Saxon G/Gifu rune.

Haligmonath rite:

Beforehand a square of turf should be loosened in the middle of the hearth and placed up side down upon the ground beside the hole it has left. A veiled effigy of the earth mother should be seated upon the Altar. All manners of fruits, grains, milk, honey, flowers and greenery should also adorn the Altar along with Red, White, black, yellow, and blue candles. The candles should be inscribed with the following runes, anointed with a mixture of milk & honey and placed in the following positions:

Red	s	placed at the southern most point of the Altar. The Sun.
White	i	placed at the northern point of the Altar. Ice.
Black	g	placed in front of the effigy. The void/ Unknown/The Mother.
Yellow	e	placed at the eastern point of the Altar Air/ The winds
Blue	l	placed at the western point of the Altar. Waters of life.

The runes spell out the word SIGEL making the element without which nothing could grow namely the power of the Sun which surrounds the goddess on the Altar.

The Lyblaeca / Lybbestre stands before the Altar and after lighting each candle says:

Hail to you, earth mother of all humankind
Feel the fire of the south.

Hail to you, earth mother of all humankind
Feel the might of the north.

Hail to you, earth mother of all humankind
May we light the darkness

Hail to you, earth mother of all humankind
Feel the breeze and warmth of the air

Hail to you, earth mother of all humankind
Feel the motion of sweet water.

And together they call you now
Together they light your way

Now turn around to the centre and say:

Together they bestow all light and life
Hail to you, earth mother of all humankind
Be you ever nurtured of the suns embrace
Be with us now as we rejoice in you're being
For Nerthus you are bold and bounteous
the gift giver
And mother to us all.

Now the Lyblaeca/Lybbestre takes up the veiled goddess on high (making sure that the veil stays in place at all times) and carries her around the hearth. As he/she does so her name is called and blessings are wished upon her and all present. All shall celebrate her with joyous hearts.

Finally she is replaced upon the Altar and all in turn shall take an offering that they have brought with them and place it in the cleared earth left by the up turned turf. Each in turn saying:

Hail to you, earth mother of all humankind
I give to thee an offering of my love
And thank you most humbly for all your gifts

Before the turf is then replaced and trodden in to place the Lyblaeca / Lybbestre shall pour the milk and honey from the Altar onto the gifts saying:

Hail to you, earth mother of all humankind
Shall you ever grow in god's embrace
Filled of food that benefits all

Hal wes þu, folde, fira modor
Beo þu growende on godes fæðme
Fodre gefylled firum to nytte

NB: the gift shall be something organic a seed, a flower or precious metal i.e. gold/silver or a heartfelt poem written on parchment or paper etc. The Nerthus effigy can be of your own choice but one made of your own design and fair hand is most beneficial. The veil can be of a floral designed but large enough to cover her completely. After the ritual the effigy should be placed upon an inner Altar and covered at all times out of sight of all. The candles should be left to go out by themselves but always be aware of them and do not leave then unattended.

Blótmónath

(Culling month November eve)

The month when offerings to the gods were made and the sick, old and weak animals culled to feed the tribe helping them survive the hardships of the approaching winter.

This festival corresponds to the Celtic Samhain and of course the feast of the dead. As the meat was offered to the gods the ancestors were called to participate in the abundance of food and drink and the celebration and bonding of the clan.

Blótmónath rite:

A fire should be lit and all present should hold a torch or lit candle. (The candle/ torch should be inscribed with the Sigil s rune.) After the affirmation of the hearth the Lyblaeca/ Lybbestre stands before the altar or in front of those congregated saying:

Winter's grip creeps ever onward
The days grow short and the nights grow grim
Together as one and with our gods
do we hold fast the breath of this dark time

Strength is needed,
strength and the broadest of backs
that can weather the loss of our sacred heat
and call the eager light to smile once more.

Fields once heavy mourn, flat and lifeless
Seed once plenty a whispered memory as the chill winds blow
And so we kindle here Sunnas fire
That cracks and spits in the face of cold fury
Warming chilled bones, a testament to all

We summon our kin to warm by the fire
To drink of our Ale and breathe the warm air
And to dwell in the bosom valued gifts of Erce
We offer the Ox, fare feast, of a fair year.

All:

Mægen ùre fana
Mægen fram ánnes
Godes mægen
Wintercyss bære wê

Might our banner
Might through unity
Gods might
Winters kiss we shall bare

After the verse has been recited all should shout and makes loud noises. All should then throw their torches/candles into the fire and with them a written note denoting some sacrifice that you will make for the benefit of you and your kin... The hearth should now be sealed. The feast now moves indoors where all should eat, drink, be snug, merry and warm!

Full Moon

(Mònaðfylen)

Many of the eight main Sabbats/festivals that are celebrated by the Lyblác tradition coincide with the nearest full moon. At this time especially if the moon is visible it creates a sense of power and of otherworldliness that ads to whatever ceremonial act is performed, bringing about an overall feeling of contentment, wonder and of spiritual connection with deity.

Every full moon should be celebrated initially to reinforce that connection with the Gods & Goddesses but also as a sort of "Thanksgiving" for the Love and kinship given by the Gods overall. It can also act as a regular moot (meeting) for a group of normally solitary Lybläc coming together not necessarily as a coven but in order to connect with the larger Lybläc Witchcraft community.

The following full moon ritual should be carried out in addition to any other rituals that coincide with the full moon and is too carried out just prior to the Ale and Bread.

Lyblaeca/Lybbestre should take up his/her staff and standing at the centre of the Hearth, strike the earth three times with the bottom of the staff and say:

Hush, hush my kindred
The light in our hearts this night
Shall match the light of the moon
It carries our dreams
and binds our Love.

He/she now points the staff at the moon saying:

Our affection and thanks we send this night
On silver wings we have charged the web
God of might, Goddess of beauty
We rejoice this night in Móna's name
So is this now and always will be.

Holding the staff by the bottom two thirds still pointing at the moon just above head height he/she starts to turn deosil turning full circle from full moon to full moon saying:

High Lyblaeca/Lybbestre: *They guard us.*

All: *Sentinels.*

Lyblaeca/Lybbestre:	*They guide us.*
All:	*The way is clear.*
Lyblaeca/Lybbestre:	*All honour to the Gods.*
All:	*Honour most profound.*
Lyblaeca/Lybbestre:	*Their Love is life.*
All:	*And all life is Love.*
All:	*So mote this be*

Obviously if you are alone then all parts are recited by you. All present should now contemplate their blessings and give thanks for all that the Gods have bestowed upon them.

Lybcraeft

Skills involved in the use of plants for magic and witchcraft

The Lybláс Wiccan (pronounced Witchan) were indeed proficient healers, seers and makers of magical charms, they were the midwives, doctors, matchmakers and users of the hidden forces of Galdra/Galdór (magic). The village Lyblaeca and Lybbestre were the Custodians of much of the hidden botanical and magical knowledge of the day concerning the powerful effects of both Witchcraft and the medicinal uses of plants, herbs and elemental forces. These Anglo-Saxon Witches could even commune with the Gods which enabled them to harness the power of the Sun, and the Moon and even the power of Mother Earth herself. The word Lyb-cræft is the Old English term meaning: One skilled in the use of drugs or charms with their usage being attributed in some way to the manipulation of magical forces. Lyb: Charm. Drug, Poison. Cræft: Art, Ability, Courage, Physical Strength, Skill, Talent.

Here follows some of the plants used in Lybcræft:

Plant/Herb	O.E. Name	Medicinal Use	Magical Use
Ash	aesc	Leaves/Laxative	Protection
Ash bark	æscrinde	Astringent	Protection
Aspen	cwicbéamrind	Bark/Worms	Anti-theft
Barley	bere	Food/Liquid Bread/Ale	Love/ Healing
Blackthorn	slahþorn	Antiseptic	Cursing

Bran	syfeᵹe	Stomach pain. Laxative	The mind
Blackberry	brembel	Bark/Leaves/ Astringent	Money/ Protection
Broadleek	bradeleac	Antiseptic	Sends evil back. Hex breaker
Burdock	clate	Leaves/root Skin irritations	Protection /ward off negativity
Centaury/ Gentian	curmelle	Blood cleansing	Purification
Clary Sage	slarege	Stomach/eyes	Longevity/ wishes
Comfrey	galluc	Wound healing	Safety during travel/ money
Cowslip	cuslyppe	Headache cure Helps sleeplessness	Restore lost youth Helps find that which is lost
Dandelion	agwyrt	Diuretic	Wish magic
Dock	ompre	Astringent	wards against Elfshot/stitch
Eyebright	eawyrt	Muscle relaxant	Spirit communication Psychic powers
Fennel	finol	Purgative	Anti Witchcraft
Foxglove	foxesclife	Heart stimulant * **[Poisonous]**	House/home Protection
Garlic	garleac	Coughs/breathing disorders	Exorcism Guards against illness
Glovewort	glofwyrt	Heart condition	Happiness and Wellbeing
Gooseberry	ᵹefeorn	Leaves/Dressing of wounds	Fertility Fishing magic
Gorse	gorst	Flowers against jaundice	Against Elves Attracts Gold

Great wort	greate wyrt	Rid one-self of warts	Love attractant Respect Loyalty
Ground Ivy	eorðifig	Strength. Indigestion	To know who attacks you by magic
Hawthorn	ðefeðorn	Weeping wounds	Ward off Witches and their craft
Heather	hæð	Aroma promotes restful sleep	Wards off passion and unwanted advances
Hellebore	tunsingwyrt	Causes vomiting and diarrhoea * **[Poisonous]**	Causes frenzy & unrest when used as an incense
Hemlock	hemlic	Sedative * **[Poisonous]**	Used in flying ointment
Hemp	hænep	Anaesthetic sleep inducing	Visions Love scrying magic mirrors
Holly	holen	To ease fevers Purgative Rheumatism	Induces wonderful dreams that may come true.
Horehound Black	Sweartehune	Eases coughs	Carried and burned against sorcery
Horehound White	hwitehune	Odour used to keep pests away	Promotes quick thinking. Wyrt of exorcism
House Leek	sinfulle	Poultice against blisters & skin irritations	Constant abundance Love
Knotweed	unfortrædde	Blood loss. Ulcers	Used for binding
Libcorn	lybcorn	Laxative. Expels worms	Against evil spirits

Lionfoot	leonfot	Root/Leaf against swellings. Also its leaves were made into cosmetics.	The wyrt of Love
Lovage	lufestice	Tea/Calmative Takes away the dimness of the eyes.	Put into baths to make one more attractive to the opposite sex.
Mallow	hocleof	Closes open wounds, cures swellings.	Protection. Love. Carried it attracts true love.
Marigold	Sigilhweorfa golde	Hair dye. Also used for chronic ulcers and varicose veins, Stimulant.	Unfaithful wives and against evil words.
Marsh Mallow	merscmergylle	Against urinary and respiratory inflammation.	Causes you to be the object of other's thoughts. Casts out Devils.
Meadow wort	medewwyrt	A corrector of the stomach. Also used for Children's diarrhoea.	Peace. Love spells. Spirit contact. Peace keeping. A happy heart.
Mint	minte	Against Fleas and other pests.	Lust. Health. Money and abundance.
Mistletoe	Mistel	Nervine. Narcotic. Epilepsy. Convulsions after eating the berries. * **[Poisonous]**	Fertility. Hunting. Carried to bring luck. Aids conception. Invisibility.
Mugwort	mucgywrt	Slight tonic properties. Palsy. Fits.	Prevents weariness. Used as a wash for crystal balls

			and magic mirrors.
Mulberry	morbeam	Used as a dye to colour other tinctures.	Used for wands it directs the Will. Protection against evil.
Toadstool [Fly agaric]	swamm	Causes hallucinations * **[Poisonous]**	Shamanic journeys. Visions.
Nettle	stiðe	Stimulating tonic. Anti-asthmatic.	Curse removal. Aids recovery. Is said to ward off ghosts.
Nut trees			
Hazel	hnutbeam	Powdered and mixed with honey for coughs	Wishes, Anti- lightning. Wisdom. Protection.
Oak	aac	Bark/strongly astringent and antiseptic.	Works against evil. Protects against harm. Planting acorns ensures money luck.
Onion	hwitleac	Antiseptic	Nailed above the door it protects against illness.
Pansy	bonwyrt	Epilepsy, Asthma	Divination. Rain maker.
Parsley	petresilige	Sweetens the breath.	Lust. Fertility. Used in purification baths. Helps to stop misfortune.
Parsnip/Carrot	feldmora	Asthma. Colic. Wind. Promotes urination.	Sex magic. Stamina problems. Fertility. Lust.

Pea	pise	Cures Warts.	Money. Love. Good fortune.
Peony	foxesgloua	* **[Toxic]**	Cures lunacy. Exorcisms
Periwinkle	parwynke	Astringent. Alleviates cramps.	Mental powers. Lust.
White Poppy	hwit popig	Sedative. Narcotic. Pain killer. * [Toxic]	Invisibility. Gives answers through dreams. Draws wealth.
Primrose	cusloppe	Rheumatism Paralysis and gout.	Keeps Witches at bay, also against any evil. Love.
Raspberry	hinbrer	Antiseptic. Astringent.	Protection. Stops the spirits of the dead coming back to haunt.
Rue	rude	Flatulence. Sciatica.	Recuperation. Improves mental processes. Hex breaker. Turns away the evil eye.
Sage	saluie	Calmative. Tonic Relieves Dyspepsia. Helps depressive states.	Longevity. Wisdom. Wish magic.
St Johns wort	corion	Expectorant. Nervine. dysentery, worms, diarrhoea, hysteria	Purification. Strength. Wards off Colds and Flu. Protects against lightning and thunderbolts.
Savory	sæperie	remedy for colic and a cure for flatulence,	Mental abilities. Tests. Success

Snapdragon	hundes heafod	Not known	Dispels negativity. Returns hexes
Sorrel	ampre	Refrigerant and diuretic. Scurvy.	Courage. Good luck.
Spikenard	nard	Ruptures. Inward wounds.	
Strawberry	streawberge	Laxative. Diuretic. A cure for rheumatic gout.	Love & Luck. Eases the pains of child-birth.
Tansy	helde	Expelling worms. Hysteria. Anti flatulent.	Long life. Stops fevers.
Thistle	ðistel	Ulcers. Diminishes discharges. A crick in the neck.	Lightning protection. Strength. Energy.
Thorn-black Sloe	slahðorn	Aperient Astringent Diaphoretic Diuretic Stomachic	Used to prick effigies. Shower of secrets. Wands and staffs of great power are made of this wood
Thorn Apple	foxes glofa * [not foxglove]	Sedative. Narcotic. {opposite to foxglove} * [Toxic]	The will. To stupefy.
Thunder Clover Ox-eye-daisy	ðunorclæfre	Asthma. Whooping cough. Nervousness.	Love & lust.
Thyme	organa	Relieves Asthma catarrh, gout.	Spirit contact. Cleansing baths. Wards against bad dreams.
Turnip	næp	Coughs and sore throat medicine.	Turns away unwanted love intentions.

Vervain	berbena	Antispasmodic. Neuralgia. Febrifuge.	Averts evil magic. Altar cleansing. Protective spirits.
Water Lilly	collencroh	Dysentery. Gonorrhoea. Inflamed skin.	Anti love spell. Wards against ghosts.
Waybread [Dock]	wegbræd [wyrte modor]	Stomach tonic. Ulcers of the eyes.	Money spells. makes conce-ption possible.
Wild celery	merece	Calmative Tonic. Aides restful sleep.	Mental ability. Tests. Lust.
Willow	weliges	Tonic. Astringent.	Healing. Wish magic. Blessings of the moon.
Woodruff	Wuduhrofe	Wound healing. Stomachic. Flavouring.	Clears the atmosphere. Wish magic. Victory.
Wormwood	Wermod	A tea relieves melancholia. Jaundice. Gout. Flavour of the drink Absinthe. * **[Poisonous]**	Visions. Clairvoyance. Psychic powers. Protects against road accidents. Love potions.
Yarrow	gearwe	Remedy for colds. Purifies the blood. Piles. Kidney infections.	Courage. Exorcism. Love. Marriage. Wards off negativity.

Tools of the trade

Ðaet cytel (The Kettle)

The Cauldron or cytel (Kettle) as used by our A.S. Witch ancestors was an integral and essential part for the working of magic a thousand years ago as it is for some today. The origin of all Kitchen Witchery, The Cauldron (ðæt cytel) not only served to combine the herbs, stones and bones and magical substances that brought unto life any magical charm, but also served as a direct route to see the future as ordained by the Gods themselves.

As the spell/charm is made and the magical recipe combined within the (cytel) the Lyblæca/Lybbestre watches the mixture carefully as it bubbles together with the water to see how well the Gods, shall ordain the magic (galdór) to work. The Gods wishes can be foretold from the froth/residue of the bubbling mixture that is "cooking" within the cauldron and should shape its self into a rune or even reveal a direct resemblance or object associated with the success or failure of the charm/spell.

[Peering over the cytel the Witch wafts away the steam/smoke and asks]

Darkest water, deepest door
Reveal thy will, of what lies fore.

Sweartwæter durudéop
Willan cyðan hwæt becuman

If the Ur ᚢ rune is seen it is as good an omen as the Gifu ᚷ rune.

Thorn ᚦ is seen as an ill omen as is Ear, Ea ᛉ

Laecseax (The Magical blade)

The magical blade used by our ancestors was called a læcseax. After the blade had been forged the handle was made of yellow horn, riveted with 3 bronze nails and inscribed with a magical runic verse said to waken it unto life when used by the Lyblæca/Lybbestre.

Such a runic charm verse could have been:

The legacy of Woden protects this work
Lyblác sige-blessed blade.

:ᚦᛖ·ᛚᛖᚷᚪᚳᚣ·ᚩᚠ·ᚹᚩᛞᛖᚾ·
ᛈᚱᚩᛏᛖᚳᛏ·ᚦᛁᛋ·ᚹᚩᚱᛣ·ᛚᚣᛒᛚᚪᚳ
ᛋᛁᚷᛖ·ᛒᛚᛖᛋᛋᛖᛞ·ᛒᛚᚪᛞᛖ:

The blade was used for all workings not just magical but was seen to transform into the læcseax or galdraecg when the verse was recited over the tool prior to magical work.

A space on the handle of the Læcseax either side can be filed flat so as to clear a place for the runic text. Once this has been done and sanded smooth an engraving tool or other sharp instrument can be used to etch in the runes. After doing so the runic script can then be coloured by rubbing a dye/ink (Blood/Red Ochre) into the groves and then re-sanded leaving it clean and free from ink and dust.

Pocca aerende (Bag/pouch/pocket of messages)

One of the ways in which fates were foretold was through the use of the "Bag of messages" or pocca ærende which hung from the girdle/belt of the Lyblác Witch.

Filled with such things as the skull of a squirrel representing the messenger that works its way up and down the world tree Yggdrasil. The bag itself was made from two pieces of cloth or fur sewn together with a ring that held the bag open.

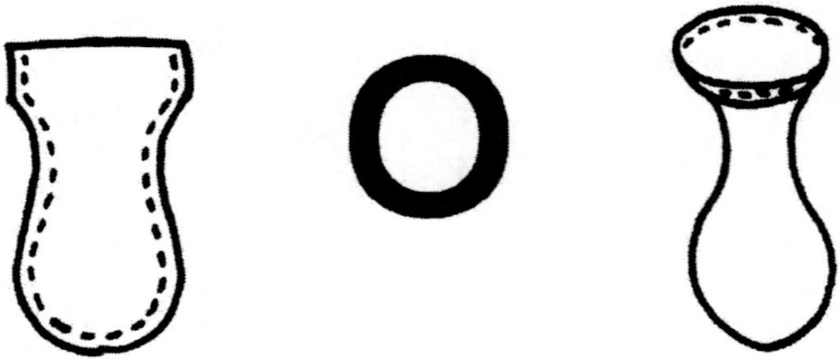

Items included in the pouch can include:

A knife/Blade. Cutting ties. A parting. Forging something new.
A pair of tweezers. Care & attention. Beware the details.

Swan feathers. Peace after turmoil. You must think long and hard.
Wood, especially if struck by lightning. Protection.
Bark. Guard. A shield. Beware that which you can not see.
Shells. Beauty. Love. Harmony.
Herbs & Roots. A cure. Magical ambition.
Red thread & twine. Possessions. Binding. Holding on to what you have.
A needle. Togetherness. A marriage.
Coins. Life & death. Children. Pregnancy. A Female.
Black & White stones. Protection. The will of the Gods.
Amber. Richness. Winning. The elderly.
A Spider. Spirits. Art & Poetry. Perseverance.
Animal bones. Loyalty. Sustenance. Well-being.
Metal nails & clippings, Brass, Bronze and silver. Wealth. Abundance.
Runes carved on wood. Each rune tells its own story.
Thorns. Enemies. Revenge. A man.
Squirrel skull. Secrets. That which is hidden. Information. The truth.

Archaeologists when excavating Anglo Saxon graves have found all of the above items inside pouches belonging to the time of the Lybliác.

The Fates

Foretelling the future is indeed an art practiced all over the world and in many cultures one way to perform such a task with the pocket of messages is so:

The recipient who would know the fates is asked either to draw an object from the bag or all of the contents are strewn upon the ground. If it is a simple answer they are looking for let them ask a single question and then pull then pull an item from the bag. For a more in-depth and detailed "Reading" when all of the bags objects have been deposited upon the earth the Lyblæca/Lybbestre should start from the centre and radiate outwards reading the fates as you go. With time and practice the fates will become a simple task to perform for anyone.

The Key

(Ðæt Cæg)

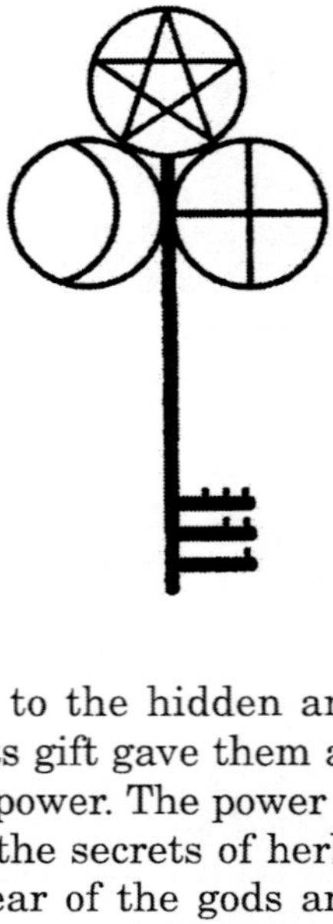

The symbol chosen for the Lybläc tradition is that of the Key. The reason for this is quite simple. As there have been so many keys found in Anglo-Saxon graves throughout England, eminent archaeologists and academics alike are convinced that these other-worldly cogent key symbols are magical & religious representations for the unlocking of spiritual and magical doorways. The Witches of the A.S. period were noted to transcend the other realms of existence and were recognisable by the wearing of such a key. The Key worn at the waist revealed to all that its owner was privy to the hidden and mystical knowledge of the gods and that its gift gave them an ultimate potency and connection to divine power. The power of the Lybläc Witch enabled them to unlock the secrets of herbs and potions and also afforded them the ear of the gods and with that came the effective ability to persuade spirits, animals and humankind to their will. For these reasons and in awe and respect of the tradition of Anglo Saxon Witchcraft we of the Lybläc have decided to wear the key as the symbol of our art and character, a recognisable token and potent sign and emblem of who and what we are.

The three circles represent the main three worlds of existence i.e. the Upper world of the gods, the Middle world of humankind, and the Lower world of the mother and the roots of the World Tree. The pentagram represents the five elements i.e. Ice, Air, Fire, Water & Earth. The sun and moon are the balancing forces of nature. The cross or Earth symbol represents our devotion to the Great Mother and her gifts.

Large, ornamental brass keys are used as they are seen as symbolic of Lybläc keys as they too open no earthly doorways.

Witch's staff

As did the Shaman and Sorcerers in many cultures throughout the world, the Lybläc Witches carried a working and ceremonial staff of power.

The staffs are made from various types of wood and are intended to represent the World Tree, giving the Witch power to commune with the Gods and journey to "other worlds" seeking information, secrets and answers to questions that could guard and guide and the whole community.

As the encroaching Christian clergy saw "their" devil in everything that they could not control the staff had to be disguised so as not to draw attention from the wrong sort of people. The staff eventually became the fabled Witches Broom as birch twigs were fastened to hide the elaborate symbols of the Witches' craft but it still retained the flying element for visiting the upper and lower mystical worlds.

The staff's decorations before the persecutions of the clergy were largely dependent upon the individual Lyblæca/ Lybbestre`s creativity and connection with the Gods. Some were very elaborate with swirls of brass; others had arrangements of Thunderstones representing the upper, middle and lower worlds of existence, and of course the Witches journeys too and from those realms. Today, as then, the Lyblác are noted for their staffs, they serve not only to show the tradition that they follow but the more intricate the design the more "Connected" with the realms and the Gods the Witch has become.

NB: Thunderstones were possibly ammonite but any sort of black, round and heavy stone will do. If you use many stones then Jet is best, as when they are varnished they look particularly good and it is also very light in weight.

Galdorsang (Magical songs)

Song of the fates

(géosceaftsang)

[To be sung over the fateful objects when looking into the future]

Mankind's fate reveal, reveal
I call the wisdom
I call the sight

Fail me not
Wide open eyes

An answer I seek
All knowing, all knowing

mannisc géosceaft cyðan cyðan
ic hátan ðæt ræd
ic hátan ðæt gesihð

ábréo_an mé ne
onhlídan eagebrád

answaru ic sécan
forwitan eall forwitan eall

Song of enchantment

(Galdorcwide)

It is stated that the Anglo-Saxon Witches of old would "Sing" things into being. These songs of enchantment were especially prevalent in conjunction with the Lyblác`s use of Lacnunga or herb magic. The songs that would "Wake unto life" the magical properties of specific plants, herbs and substances, were always song three times over. The Witches' object of choice being infused or conjured with the intent, purpose and magical power through the singing of such a mighty and commanding galdorcwide or enchanting Song. If it fell to the Lybiác to help heal someone who had sustained injury, either through, accident, general sickness or fighting, the Lyblaeca/ Lybbestre would not only enchant the healing herbs, but also use their bewitching song to enchant the individuals themselves. Often by singing into his/her mouth, over his/her body or even directly into the wounds of the patient. Again the enchantment being sung three times over each specific herb, person or wound.

Wyrtgaldor

(Herb enchantment)

When harvesting the herb, and at the point of use, sing the following:

Ùplicewyrt min cwide gehìeran
galdorléoþ abannan ic
fram gesælð fyllan
nerthus beháten
geséon áweccan

Supreme herb hear my song
A spell I summon
Of good fortune fulfil
Promise of Nerthus
Behold I call you out.

The Smiðsang
(The maker's song)

Born of the mother this holy fruit
Of leaf and bud and stem
Of knowledge sought
This rune is worked
A gift to God and men

Blood is binding
Bless-ed blood
Rune might whispered wrought
Holy sisters
Weave the fates
Favour this holy work.

Interestingly enough the word men or man in our ancient past is not necessarily masculine. The old A.S. word "*mennisc*" means person or human, the word for women stemming from "*wifmann*" meaning wife person or weave person. Also another interesting word for wife in Anglo Saxon times was *cwèn* the origins of the word Queen. So as the song refers to "God and men" it simply means The Gods and humankind.

Another Smiðsang spoken softly over the finished rune/s can be directly used to empower or charge as follows.

***** "Woden, Woden rûnhearra**
þin galdor onlænan --- to min willan
onwæcnan mihgtigrûn --- ðæt webb gebìgan
gesceaft ést
gesælðgewinnan."*

** " Woden, Woden, Rune Master*
Lend your magic --- to my will
Awake mighty rune --- the web shall bend
fates favour
good fortune win"

Magic from the well of Wyrde (The Mothers)

At the roots of the world tree Yggdrasil, three wise and mighty sisters: Urð, Verðandi and Skuld known as "The Mothers" in Anglo Saxon England maintain the multiverse by weaving and manipulating the Web of Wyrd.

A mixture of grey clay & water covers the roots of the great Ash. The mixture is drawn from the Well of Wyrd by the sisters (collectively known as the Nornir/Norns) and administered to the roots of the tree to guard and protect them so that they do not wither or rot. The Tree itself represents the deeds of the present. The Well is a representation of the past and the sisters are charged with bringing those past deeds into the future, which shall form the basis for all forthcoming deeds.

As all is written within the Web, when "Magic" is performed the Web has been "warped" or "stretched" causing a desired event to occur. But when this occurs it will cause another reaction in the future.

Rune: ᚨ Responsibility, Past acts, persuasion, Delusion. ᚾ Need

Tree: Ash

Urð, Verðandi and Skuld can be invoked for:

To bend the web of life for all that you may wish to change especially for the haunting of past deeds but beware:

"The deed may come back to bite you on the backside".

Spoken/Written charms

Written in runes (the longer the poem the better) the spell is chanted out loud and often marked at the end in some way with the Gifu rune ᚷ

To banish illness

[The following verse should be written in red ink or red Ochre then recited out loud over the person who shall receive the healing. Whilst doing this a black stone/pebble taken from the seashore is given to the recipient of the charm. All evil/illness is then loaded into the stone, and then the stone is wrapped in the verse and buried]

Of heaven I charm
Seek the protection of Nerthus
Of Sun of Moon and Gods embrace
Granting gifts the healing words,
chain quickened hands to cure evils breath
From the highest cry, to the deepest sleep
Ward and watch the ill wind grows silent
These runes I have wrought on blackest stone
A halt to all evil, forged of no bridel
The raven heard, as did the bear
In fish and fowl the word craft ripens
Night holds no fear the doors are bolted
All illness is driven out
This magick is spoken.

fram heofon ic besingan
secan nerthus fæðm
fram sunne fram mona ond godeshrepian
alyfan gifu se hàlwende word
racente snele hand yfulæþm gebetan
fram heáh wépan ond slùmadéop
hyrde wacian _aet adligwind in swigian wexan
geðrùen rùnstæf on swearte stán
eall yfell hìe forstopian nábrìdel sléan
þæt hræfn forewitan bera forewitan
wordcræft gerìpian In fisc ond fugol
niht warian duru fæstan
eall leger geùtian
þis galdorword spræc

Charm against Love/Sexual bewitchments

From an Apple tree, cut a small Y shaped branch (About 12 inches in overall length) and then proceed to hollow out the stem part of the branch making it like a large straw. Make sure that you hollow out from the bottom of the V to the bottom of the I. when the task has been completed take the branch to a natural clear/clean spring. (It could be possible to use bottled spring water but actually going to the spring works much better) Let the natural spring water pour through the branch collecting the flow in an earthenware jug or glass jar reciting the following verse as you do so.

Changing waters, through this magical tool I do now pour thee
Nourishment of the mother bring sense where sense once was
Let nature's virtue banish all bewitchment
Return to just feelings
Let go of all torments
Turn back to right delight and joyous days

Secure the vessel now full of water. Take the vessel home and, starting on a Friday, use the spring water inside (pouring it through the branch as you did at the spring) when you make the first drink of the day, once again recite the verse over the water as it flows into the cup/kettle. Give the drink to the one who has been bewitched. This should be done for nine consecutive days whilst the recipient knows nothing of the act.

[The verse could be written in runes on parchment in red ink/blood mixed with some of the water and placed beneath the recipient's bed without their knowledge.]

NB Beware of any natural spring water as it may possibly be polluted. An alternative is to buy bottled spring water.

Good fortune

Whilst out walking, one should pick a leaf from an Ash tree to ensure good fortune reciting the following verse as you place it in your pocket:

Tree of Ash a leaf I take
A gift of luck my fortune makes
Should no good blessings follow me
The will of the Gods I bestow on thee.

Æsc án léaf ic niman
gesælðond gódnes bringan
gif ná fremu sculan éow giefan
godescwide sculan æfterhyrgan

[Ash a leaf I take
Good fortune and goodness bring

If no luck shall you give
Gods will, shall follow]

Blessing the mead

Before drinking mead one should make a toast so that maybe, just a drop could be of the original brew that will turn you into a world famous poet.

Bless-ed mead,
the fires of inspiration light.
the word gift give
Sweet language of the poet
Protector, breath of Woden
Word craft that I may steal

Gesælig medu
ðæt inbryrdnes fýr léoht
ðæt wordgift giefan
swéte geðéodescop
léodgebyrga æþm framWoden
wordcræft ðæt ic stelan mótan

Magical Clay Dolls

(þæt gelìcnes)

In Anglo Saxon England in the 10th century, a woman and her son were tried for pushing nails into a clay effigy of a man. The lady was subsequently drowned under London Bridge but her son escaped to become an outlaw. This shows that magic and Witchcraft were being practised over a thousand years ago and that the use of "Clay Dolls" or þæt gelìcnes (The likeness) was used in Anglo Saxon England to perform sympathetic magic. The Romans also used clay effigies well before this time. These clay dolls into which they would place magical scrolls containing powerful verses that have been said to entice shy, potential sex partners not to be able to resist the wishes or affections of the spell caster. These dolls were then hidden in secret places to work their charms and many have been subsequently re-discovered by modern-day archaeologists. The finding of such dolls implies that the use of sympathetic magic within the British Isles well over a thousand years ago seems to have been much more wide-spread than was first thought! Unlike our Witch ancestors of old, it is easy for any of us today to obtain such materials as air-drying clay, and as such the making or forming of any likeness/effigy of whoever or whatever is not likely to cause any worry at all.

To get a Lover

Obtain some air drying clay and form some of it into a figure. Now before the clay dries inscribe in red ink/blood a runic charm onto a long thin strip of paper i.e;

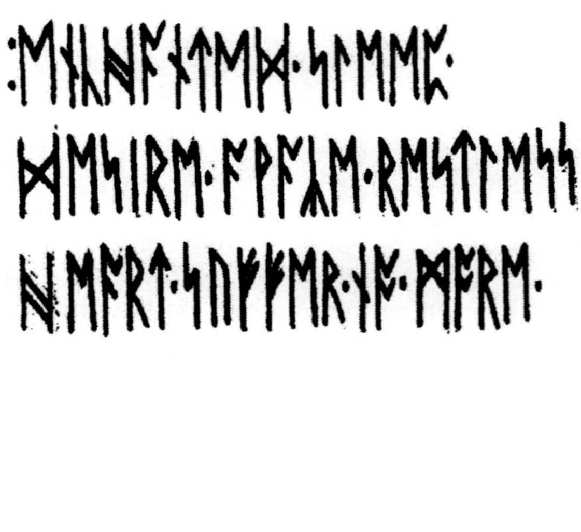

[It is also a good idea to add your name]

Enchanted sleep, desire awake
Restless heart, suffer no more.
Favour, delight, and love.
My will be done.

besingan slæpan - lust onwæcnan
unstille heorte ðowian nàmà
wylm - wynn - ond lufu
min willan
béon

Roll the strip into a small tube/scroll. Now make a hole in the clay doll where the heart should be. Place the scroll inside the doll and as you do so recite the A.S. verse three times and envisage your desire happening. After this, softly blow life into the heart of the effigy. Put clay over the top of the scroll, filling in the hole and then smooth it over. The effigy should now be placed with some pictures or picture (of the sort of person you wish to attract) in a secret place; (If you live alone a shoebox under your bed works fine) you need not ever disturb the doll again unless you have attracted "the one" for

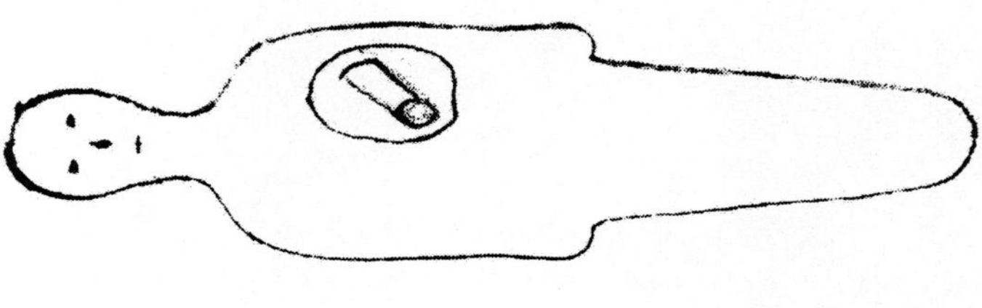

you. When the desired effect has been achieved all you need to do is to take the doll, break it open, then destroy the scroll inside. The variations to this sort of sympathetic magic are seemingly endless.

Obviously it is easy to add genitalia, which would determine the sex of the clay doll, and this would definitely add to the overall effect. But, if there was a specific person in whom you were interested then a photograph of the face of that person stuck onto the doll would be even better. Now as the doll sleeps it will attract that which is desired.

Of Enchantments

To get someone to fall in love with you:

In order to "enchant" a suitable partner you should firstly buy the person to be enchanted a cup (*lìð) or drinking vessel of some kind. Pour some sort of beverage into the vessel Tea, Coffee, Mead, Wine etc, so that it is nearly full to the brim. Now take a silver pin and prick the little finger of your left hand until you draw blood. Now hold the now bloodied finger underneath the vessel moving three times in a circular clockwise direction. Visualise the one who is to be enchanted doing and saying what you would like them to do towards you, after the third rotation sing:

* ***lufiend abidan niðeweard***

Hold the finger to the side of the vessel and say:

* ***weaxaþ lufian andland***

Now hold the finger above it and say:

* ***bufan þæt hreðe rípe***

Dropping three small drops of blood inside the beverage say:

* ***ond lufugál Innan longað***

Make the sign of the Ing rune above the vessel in the air. ᛝ

Give the full vessel to the person whom you wish to enchant making sure that they drink every drop. They should soon be unable to get you out of their mind and may well seek to take things further.

[The Ing rune above symbolising the act of male/ female copulation]

*Underneath a lover waits

*Besides grows love

*Above ripens the heart

*And inside drunk of love, longing

* Lìɤ . A cup.

* Our ancestors saw no conflict in turning one's thoughts to love or "manipulating" the favours of another.

NB: In this day and age actually dropping your blood into the cup may well constitute breaking some law somewhere? Therefore substitutions are acceptable but may not work as well?

To turn a barren womb fertile

This enchantment sounds a little insensitive but you have to realise the way in which barrenness was seen a thousand years ago. The one who would bear a child makes a chalk bead (signifying mother's milk and found in many A.S. children's graves) this she places on a red cord. She then goes to the grave of a recently deceased child wearing about her neck the chalk bead on the thread. She wears no undergarments underneath a long flowing gown. Taking the necklace she places it into her right hand she then "jumps" over the grave (from right to left) transferring the single beaded necklace over to her left hand then says:

***** *sárlic bearn diend náht***

She then transfers the bead back to her right hand, walks around the top of the grave and repeats the jumping and bead switching once again. This time she should say:

***** *meolc genòg rípe cépan***

She now repeats the process again this time saying:

***** *tó mé nú cuman ond þin sárnes ende***

She now stands with one foot either side of the grave. She then kneels still with legs apart then sits back on her heels making sure that her dress flows out around her in a wide circle. She now says:

***** *Nerthus eorðen mòdor þin earm geopenian***
læt mìn cwiða mid cild full wesan

It is important that the woman's vagina touches the earth as she recites this. Now as she kneels she should take the single beaded necklace and holding it in her right hand press it against her stomach. She now places her left hand over her right and says:

**** bearn for éow án cradol ic ágan***
cáf ond waerm luflic þin stede
in mé weaxen swæs næft cild
gròwende lif mé lytel ác
lufiendlic lufiendlic
uncer ánnes

She now should make the sign of the Beorc rune ᛒ with the bead on her stomach.

She should then take some soil from the grave and place it with the single beaded necklace in her home. If the goddess is willing, the womb will bear fruit.

Interpretation:

- Sad baby, suckling not
- Milk enough ripe awaits
- To me now come and end your sorrow

- Nerthus earth mother, your arms open
- Let my womb with child full be

- Baby for you a cradle I have
- Strong and warm lovely your home
- In me grows beloved child of need
- Growing life, my little Oak!
- Loving, Loving
- Our covenant

As with all magical verse it can be recited in Modern English. Try the Old English word version the words have a positive resonance, as does the Lybläc Call and when delivered properly can give you goose bumps and a real feeling of connection!

Charm against an enemy

Tip a mixture of various sized thorns into a pot and slowly warm them through (do not burn them). Whilst the thorns are still hot tip them into a bag and take them outside, finding a secluded spot. Now stand facing the direction of the person who would wish you harm. Take the bag and tip some of the thorns onto the ground as you do so stamp your foot eight times onto the ground saying:

"......Name.......name..... þin nama ábannan
prician ðæt ðorn
_in flæsc ábìtan
friðoðstanden
ræst infinden ðu ná mára"

"......Name......Name......your name I call
prick the thorn
into your flesh it bites
peace is lost
rest no more shall you find"

Now take the rest and throw them in the his/her direction saying:

**** "blind ond feascéaft éower craeft***
gehéawan belifd"

"blind and wretched is your craft
cut down, lifeless"

Now take one of the thorns and scratch the name of the wrong-doer into the earth.

Over the name draw a gate, then the Thorn rune ᚦ after which you should push the thorn that you have used to mark the ground with into the middle of the name, and leave it there. It is done!

A charm for confidence

Take the herbs Thyme & Wode (Organa & Wad) dry them out and then grind them together into a fine powder. Take half the powder and mix it with a small amount of laguðunor water that was collected during a thunderstorm. When you are ready, stand naked and mix the ingredients together in a small bowl. As you do so sing the following out loud:

"þegnlic standen ðæt homer mægen
sigelêoð ond lofsang
gæst framðunnar
min blòd drêfan
gefæst ferð ond gefæst hand."

"Noble stands the hammers might
song of victory and song of praise
spirit of Thunor
my blood stirs up
steady of mind and steady hand."

Take your finger and dip it into the mixture, now mark the sign of the hammer in the middle of your chest and on each arm. Put the bowl down and light a charcoal block. Now place the block in a dish, which has already been a quarter filled with sand. Place them both on the ground before you. Now sprinkle the rest of the "dried" mixture onto the charcoal block. At this stage you should be very careful as you stand above the smoke (do not put too much mixture on the block so as to make too much smoke!) Envisage the power of Thunor`s might surging through your veins. Sing the song once more whilst slightly stamping your feet in a slow repetitive fashion repeating the verse as many times as you need to.

NB: It is a good idea to memorise the song and whenever you feel that you are in need of confidence sing it out, the louder the better.

A charm against those who disgrace and are dishonourable

Take a piece of cloth about 6 inches square. Place in the centre of the cloth an item from those that have disgraced or dishonoured you. Go to a crossroads late at night taking with you the cloth and item, pick up about half a handful of dirt, place the dirt together with the item in the centre of the cloth bringing all four corners together and then tie securely with some cord. Being very careful so as not to be seen, throw the package that you have just made onto the ground and then stamp down hard on top of it saying:

fela unlif ábídan beornas árléas
mánfremmend
mánfremmend
fram ðylc hearm sculan þin dægan cwiðan
ná mára heofonléot geséon
ábídan þu ðæt dòmbyre
for cùðist þin nama fáncenful
féasceaft ond forbiernan

many deaths await dishonourable men
evildoer
evildoer
from such hurt your days lament
no more heavens light see
await you the doom time
for clearly is your name deceitful
miserable and consumed by fire

NB: If you notice it says "dishonourable men" but men in this instance means both Men & Women, all humankind. Stamp as many times as you see fit.

Wet the "New born"
(waeten ðaet níwgeboren)

When the "New born" arrives home (or is a few days old) and after all are OK, the husband with other family members "Wet" the baby's head. The toasts of Ale or Mead are drunk each time the husband/lover announces the boasts, which are as follows:

Husband's boasts

Husband: *A time of smiles and of life everlasting*

All: ***Welga lif fyllu gebéot***

Husband: *A time of happiness and of love commanding*

All: ***Welga lif fyllu gebéot***

Husband: *A gift from the Gods our kin ever joining*

All: ***Welga lif fyllu gebéot***

Husband: *Of well full hearts and pride in our standing*

All: ***Welga lif fyllu gebéot***

Husband: *Hail to this new life, an ancestor returning*

All: ***Welga lif fyllu gebéot***

Husband:	*In strength and honour our line never ending*
All:	***Welga lif fyllu gebéot***
Husband:	*Health, wealth and joys beholding*
All:	***Welga lif fyllu gebéot***
Husband:	*Precious of purpose a wife's full loving*

The toast, which contains eight separate mouthfuls of Ale, represents the never-ending knot or the two conjoining circles of both male and female energies that went into creating the offspring.

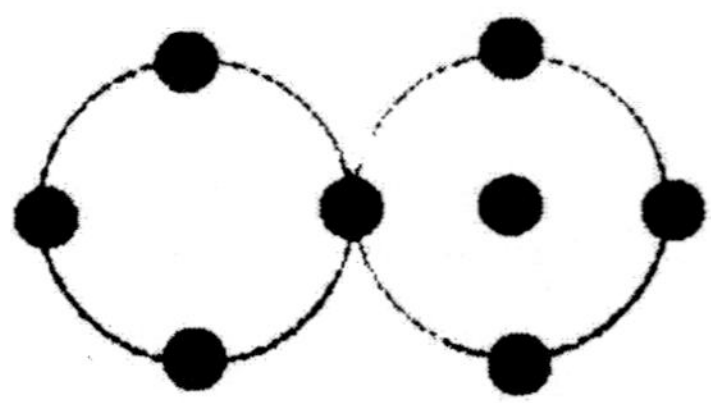

Welga lif
Hail Life

Fyllu gebéot
Fullness promise

Appeasing spirits (gást geswefian)

As we all know too well prevention is better than cure, so the Appeasing of spirits (Of whom it was said they were the main cause for many of humankind's ills) was carried out by our ancestors, and seen as a very practical way of ensuring health, wealth and happiness in a somewhat frightening world of gods, demons and magic. The acts of appeasement/ sacrifice were not only performed for the benefit one's self, but to aid and sustain the greater community as a whole. The gást geswefian or the "putting the ghost to sleep" rite, acted to lull or to calm those entities that could and would cause mischief and mayhem if left to their own devices.

House Wights

Every home has its own house wight, which gives personality and character to the house/home, influencing the occupants in many areas. In order to make a house feel like a home one should celebrate the spirit of the house by placing offerings at the highest point of the dwelling. For example up inside the attic, loft or roof space. The day that you move to your new premises becomes the birthday of the house wight. Before you settle into your new home take a saucer or small plate and place upon it, a piece of bread, some salt, and a small cup of milk mixed with honey. Go to the highest point of your house (If you live in a flat or apartment find an out-of-the-way place that does not get disturbed) taking with you all of the items. Holding the saucer/plate in both hands say aloud:

"I call to the spirit of this house / home
This offering I bring as a sign of respect
May my / our laughter echo in your heart
And I / We shall live in the light of your embrace
Bring health, wealth and happiness".

gesundfulnes -- æht -- éadignes

Health -- Wealth -- Happiness

[Re-do this every year on the birthday of the house, or at the main festivals. The birthday can also be any day of choice. Do not use too much milk & honey, as it will take on a sour smell as it breaks down]

Land Wights

There have been many finds throughout the wilds of British Isles and Ireland where a stone has been carved with an indentation/bowl within a spiral pattern. This bowl-like feature is where people would make offerings to Wights, sprites and spirits over the many centuries of our history and is a widespread indication of the appeasement of these supernatural beings. Find a secluded spot, preferably on high ground. If you know of a site where there are already offering stones, then use the bowls provided as they are proved centres of spiritual activity. Otherwise find a stone that feels right. Taking firstly the milk and honey, tip 80% of the contents of the cup onto the stone saying:

"I call upon the spirits of this place
This offering I bring as a mark of respect
May love and laughter echo in this place
Filled with light in the mothers embrace
Be nourished and filled a gift of frith
Lend health, lend wealth, and lend all happiness".

gesundfulnes -- æht -- gesælð

Now take up the bread and tear it into roughly four equal sections. Dip each piece of bread in turn, into the leftover milk & honey mixture and then into the salt. Place the first piece onto the stone outside of the bowl/stone's centre, pointing north saying in either Modern English or A.S.:

"God-fearing"
godfyrt

Placing the second piece on the south side and say:

"For magical might"
æfter galdocræft

The next piece place on the eastern side saying:

"For desire and will"
æfter lust ond willa

The last piece should now be placed on the bowl's western side saying:

"For all that is restless".
for eall unstille

NB: The offerings should be made at the eight main festivals.

Summoning (ábannan)

Sound was of the utmost importance to our Anglo Saxon forbears. The magic/galdór inherent in their language would have always been used whenever a charm was created to bring a desire into being or spell "unto life". When the Lyblaeca/Lybbestre wanted someone to contact them he/she faced the direction where the intended resided or is at that particular time and "Sang to the winds" the song was the name of the intended person with which contact was to be established.

The ábannan song should be performed in a soft and melodic voice, almost a whisper and song with total intent and belief. The song can be as follows:

......Name......

gelýstan gelýstan
ðu ic ábannan
Wind æboda
Æberan min néodlaðu

......Name......

Listen Listen
You I call
Wind messenger
Carry my wish

Life Path (bládweg)

To see signs of the path that you shall tread, go out alone into the country taking with you a new and empty pocca ærende (Bag of messages)

Call upon the gods especially Erca the earth mother to lay "Truths" in your way. Then you shall gather all that has been placed in your path to show you the way of your future. Objects may include Stones, Feathers, Seeds, Bones, all of which you will be able to interpret. From these spirit messages and from their colours, patterns, symbols and markings you will be able to get a good idea of the path that you shall tread.

To gain Success (geblaedfaestnes habben)

To ensure success in the home find yourself three stones, your best bet is to find some flat pieces of flint about the size of half the length of your thumb. Such stones are easy to find on a beach on any coastline. Once these have been obtained inscribe the (ᛟ) Èþel rune upon each of the three stones. On the reverse side inscribe your own family mark/motto or name. Prick your finger and rub your own blood into the inscriptions on both sides of the stones. Now take the stones together with a tool such as a trowel with which you can dig a small hole. Starting in the north and anything up to a mile away from your home and facing the direction of your dwelling, kneel and dig a hole into the earth which should be no deeper than a hand length. Once you have completed the task take one of the three stones holding it in both hands and say:

Èþel Èþel forgiefan þæt galdor
Geblædfæstnes min behydig
éadwíc éadwíc

Èþel Èþel bestow your magic
Success my intent
An abode of prosperity

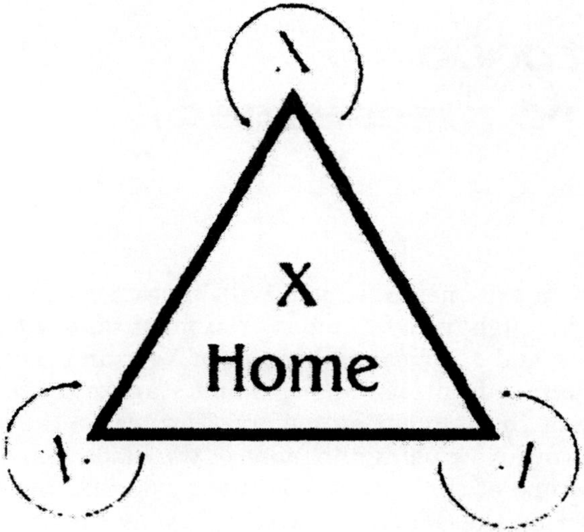

Place the rune with the upper most point of (ᛟ) facing the direction of your home, place it into the hole and cover with earth.

Proceed with the other two "Holes" and runes in a triangular shape around your home. Making sure that the rune faces "Homewards" each time; this should ensure a very prosperous home.

Gástboda
(Spirit messenger)

To receive Spirit messages you will have to go to a selected grave on the night of a full moon. You must take with you two 6 inch long and 1 inch round pieces of Yew, and a very sharp blade. Stand in front of the grave and start to carve the first of the pieces into a point at one end. Now carve the second in the same way. Now using the point of the blade mark the first flat top of one of the staves with the nýd rune, on the other stave inscribe the ác rune. Now prick your finger and mark both of the runes in blood. Taking the first stave "Plant it" in the ground where the heart of the deceased would be. The second stave should be placed in the same manner but six inches to the left of the first and about three inches below. As you are doing this recite the following "Spirit song" (gástgaldor) over the grave.

Slumagæst onwæcnan
Ic ---Your name--- ***lybläc freá***
godescyn -- háten eow
slumagæst drefen fram neðan beamore
þin nama cnáwan Ic
Soðic sècan

Sleeping spirit awake
I ---Your name --- *master / mistress of Lybläc*
And Gods kindred, call you.

Stir sleeping spirit from beneath the roots of trees
Your name I know
I seek the truth

The voice of the occupant of the grave is said to answer your questions!

When you have heard all you want to simply say whilst removing the staves:

ræst ræst ginæst gást
slæp þæt lang slæp

Sleep, sleep generous spirit
Sleep the long sleep.

NB; the staves can be used time and time again but the marking of each rune with blood should be re-done each time

Harii/Wuotanes her (Invocation of the Lord Woden's Army of the Dead)

A devoted "bodyguard" was formed to protect the Lord Woden by warriors whose strength, loyalty and ferocity was legendary amongst the Germanic tribes. The Harii, or hellish apparition as Tacitus called them, painted their bodies and shields with a dye, as did the Celts. The dye used by the Harii was mixed with the ash of battle fires in order to blacken their bodies and make them look like living corpses. Whenever the Harii went into conflict they would choose the half-light of dusk so they would appear like ghostly spectres upon the field of battle. This resulted in the opposing force being "Beaten" before they had even started. Amongst other reasons behind their fear and dread of this horrific army of darkness was the fact that it was said that intermingled within this mighty flesh and blood bodyguard of the Lord Woden were the souls of those already slain upon another field of blood. Ferocious and magical ghost warriors that could not be beaten or slain a second time around. An unstoppable army of the dead unyielding and frenzied that wailed a terrifying cry of an almighty force and power that could never fail or be vanquished.

[The following invocation should never be taken lightly. It is very rarely used, as the consequences can be dire]

Items needed: Herbs, Woad, Mugwort, a bowl, Ale or mead, a sword, an axe and a drum. Blood or blood substitute, a drinking horn and a blanket.

The Lyblaeca/Lybbestre would not normally ever need to work this charm/invocation for him/herself as they are already protected from harm by the gods. It may however be performed for another against his/her foe as a last resort when all else has failed.

Beforehand a sufficient amount of dye/brew using Woad/Wad, Water, Mugwort and Blood is to be made. The Lyblaeca/ Lybbestre shall kindle a fire in a secluded place where you will not be disturbed. The person who needs the invocation should be naked under a thin loosely fitting robe. There should be a sword and an axe placed upon the Altar. The petitioner of the charm should be seated before the fire. After the normal hearth observances have been made the Lyblaeca/ Lybbestre stands before the hearth and takes up a burning branch from the fire. Taking the burning branch he/she moves counter clockwise around the outer edge of the circle. On reaching the Altar the branch is extinguished in the bowl containing the dye mixture he/she says in a loud and forceful voice:

Fire and ash, wort and blood
I summon the armies of the dead.

The branch now cool is to have some of the soot and ash washed off in the dish with the dye mixture, the branch can then be returned to the fire.

The petitioner is now given a draft of Ale, which is "downed" in one gulp.

Another branch is now taken from the fire this time moving clockwise around the circle the Lyblaeca/Lybbestre stands once more before the Altar and again quenches the fire of the branch in the dye mixture saying:

Hordes of horror, the faithful slain
I rouse you forth, rise once again.

Once more the branch is extinguished and "Washed" then returned to the fire. Again the draft of Ale is given to the petitioner and quickly swallowed.

The Lyblaeca/Lybbestre now takes the sword from the Altar and moves it through the flames saying:

This blade sings the song of fire
Strong and true soon quenched with blood

Some ash is then scooped up with the tip of the blade and together with the blade is dipped into the brew and stirred. The sword is then given to the petitioner in his/her right hand. Yet another draft of Ale/Mead is given to them and swiftly drunk.

Now the Axe is taken from the Altar and moved through the flames saying:

To fell a flame takes the best of magic
To fan the flame takes nought but courage.

Again some ash is scooped and together both axe and ash is immersed into the liquid. The petitioner is then given the axe in his/her left hand and the Lyblaeca/Lybbestre offers another draft without the recipient touching the horn with their hands. The ale is once more drunk straight down.

The petitioner then stands.

As the Lyblaeca/Lybbestre moves towards the Altar to fetch the blood, ash and wort mixture the petitioner stands and places the sword and axe in front of them and he/she discards their robe. The dye/mixture is now offered, the petitioner takes the offering dipping a hand into the bowl and then proceeds to smear his/her body from head to toe with the infusion. After this has been accomplished another draft of ale/mead is given and once again quickly drunk. The sword and axe are then taken up again by the petitioner and held aloft then following after the Lyblaeca/Lybbestre the petitioner should recite in a loud and forceful voice:

heolstorfierd unlif geðrùen
þù ic abannan

cwalu hord
mé nù gewrecan

Dark army, forged of death
You I summoned

Hordes of destruction
Avenge me now

The Lyblaeca/Lybbestre now starts to sound the drum in a slow resonating loud beat. Soon the dark hordes are said to appear which in turn shall cause "The Madness" to overtake the petitioner. Then shall the besmeared petitioner become part of the Army of the Dead for as long as it takes to "Visit" those who would and are doing harm to the petitioner. It is possible that the petitioner could fall in a dizzied faint so it would be prudent that all care should be taken to ensure the safety of the petitioner and of course yourself! When the job is done the Ghost Horde will dissipate by itself. A blanket should be wrapped around the petitioner before the hearth is sealed. The above verse can be recited several times one after the other if so wished.

Blood: This can be substituted with red ochre

Mugwort: Drives off devilish possessions and halts all evil Leechdoms turning back the gaze of all whom are evil.

Woad: Bringer of the "Madness" wort of Intoxication and Frenzy.

Sending the Hammer (Homergaest)

Sometimes the need arises to halt the onslaught of another's malicious tongue or actions. One remedy for this is as follows:

Acquire the symbol of Thunor/Thor. Take the hammer in your left hand and close your eyes (If the hammer is around your neck you have no need to take it off) now see in your mind's eye that your right hand holds a full sized Ghost or Spirit hammer. Get ready to throw the spirit hammer, but just before you do, envisage your adversary and say out loud:

I summon here the hammer's might
Thunderer, Thunor`s strength I call to aid
Thus so shall you...name... *reap the justice of the gods*
For the hammer wards my stead
It guards the righteous

[Now throw the spirit hammer in the direction of your foe. See its devastating effects.]

See another spirit hammer appear in your hand and say:

I summon now storm and fury
Lightning, Thunor`s protection I call to aid
Thus so shall you...name... *reap the wrath of my kindred*
For my shield is that of the hallowed
It forges cruel fire against all evils.

[Once more throw the spirit hammer in the direction of your foe. See its devastating effects]

See the third and final hammer appear in your hand and say:

I summon now rain and wild winds
Potent Power, Thunor`s breath I call to aid
*Thus so shall you…*name…*reap the reward of the unworthy*
For my oath is to the gods
And forever they deliver safe harbour to me and mine.

[Again, throw the spirit hammer in the direction of your foe. See its devastating effects. The above can be used anytime but should always be said with the greatest of conviction.]

Making a Lybläc Staff

As has been said before the individual staffs that were used by the Lybläc were used not only to transverse the worlds, but as a way that others could recognise the Lyblaeca/Lybbestre as Priest and Priestess of the Gods. The Lybläc staff was carved and patterned in such a way as to represent the Lower, Middle and Upper realms of Magic, Humankind of course the world of the Gods.

Acquiring the wood

The wood that you use can be from whatever tree you think suitable for your needs. I have found Cherry birch with a natural Honeysuckle twist to be not only very easy to work but it also "stains" really well to look very old and effective. Once you have chosen the wood for your staff and before you cut it from the mother tree, make an offering at the roots of the tree for this gift of power that you, the earth and the wood are going to create.

Placing "Nourishment" at the roots of the tree you may say the following:

Strong tree, mighty but yielding
A gift of thy wood I ask
My claim, one of Nerthus blood
Your succour and aid to me an unwavering duty

This righteous foundation
and mark of our kindred
shall be the banner, which is Lybĺác
forged shall it now be,
of our craft, and of all virtues and cunning.

Worthy be --- mighty tree
Worthy be --- strong staff
Worthy be --- Witch of Lybĺác

Weorðbeon --- mihtig bèam
Weorðbeon --- swi_ stæf
Weorðbeon --- lybĺác wicca

[NB "Nourishment" can be an offering of silver or something to feed the tree.]

Staff Symbolism

The lower part of the staff representing the lower world of the Norns and the roots of the world tree Yggdrasil can be decorated with interlacing weave swan patterns which depict the very first swans that swam around the roots of the great tree and the intertwining roots themselves. The Lybĺác of old also used patterns of swirling brass. This effect can be obtained by using brass nails hammered into place upon the staff in swirling ring patterns.

The middle section of the staff represents the twists and turns and complexities of the lives of humankind. The top of third of the staff represents the world of the Gods. Its design should be of an elaborate nature, befitting its representation in honour of their might and main. The top can be covered in a leather sleeve held in place by large brass upholstery nails. A large brass animal head can adorn the very top of the staff. In the past I have used a pewter Ram's head, a brass Stag's head, a Bull's head and a brass Eagle with wings outstretched. All of which looked very pleasing to the eye and most effective. When you eventually finish your staff and have consecrated it as a magical tool it will prove not only to be a work of art, but serve to be an object of power which if used as our ancestors did, could be a means by which it may be possible to traverse the hidden worlds of all existence.

I have put a few suggestions together here as to what sort of patterns/symbolism one could use to adorn parts of your Lybläc staff. There are many weave patterns available which can be easily transferred from paper to staff by using a pencil and a little imagination.

Photocopy your design. Cut it out and go over it with a pencil. Now transfer the design to the staff placing the pencilled inside face down on the wood (You can secure it at this point if you wish with some sticky tape). Now take the pencil and go over the outline of your design making sure to use enough pressure to transfer your design to the wood. After you have removed the paper your design should have been copied onto your staff. At this stage you can heat the screwdriver over a flame getting the flat metal end glowing orange. Being extremely careful, follow the outline of your design, burning a little way into the wood. Once you have finished make sure that you quench the screwdriver under running water to cool it off. A good idea is to stain the wood a different colour to the burned-in design; this gives a good contrast and makes the design stand out.

Creating Your Work of Art

Once the wood has been acquired and left to lie flat in a cool dry place (note it can take up to at least one year for the wood to dry out properly) it is important to note that when drying the wood the bark should be left untouched so as to prevent the wood splitting during the process. Once the staff has dried out sufficiently all you will need will be a utility knife (with several blades) a small flat-head screwdriver (that can withstand the high temperatures whilst being heated and used to burn the patterns into the wood) and of course some good quality sandpaper.

After the wood has dried out sufficiently cut off all of the bark. Now mark off three sections symbolising that will come to symbolize the upper, middle and lower worlds. (The middle section should be about 17 inches 40cm in length and carved with spirals to symbolize the twists and turns of Human existence.) Taking your utility knife cut a ridge a few millimetres deep into the staff at the marked points. After the ridges have been cut, mark the middle section of the staff with a pencil in a spiralled fashion.

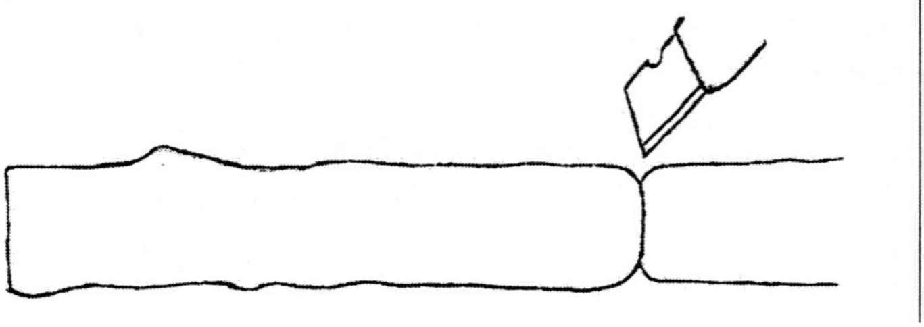

You should be exceptionally careful with the utility blade even to the point of wearing protective gloves. You must change the blade regularly. A blunt blade can be more lethal than a new one.

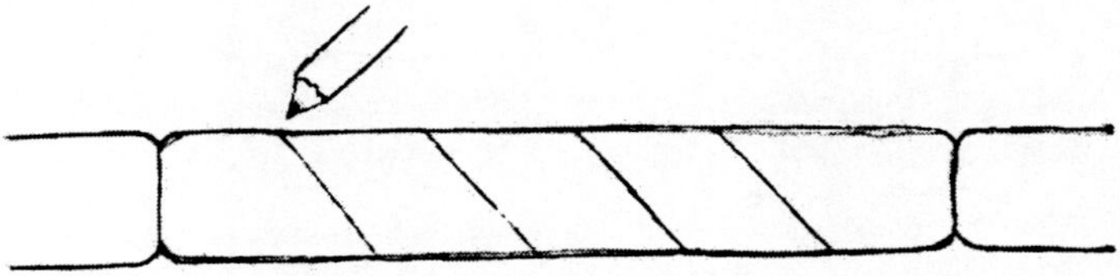

Now take a small saw and following the spiralled pencil line, saw into the wood to the depth of about 5 millimetres.

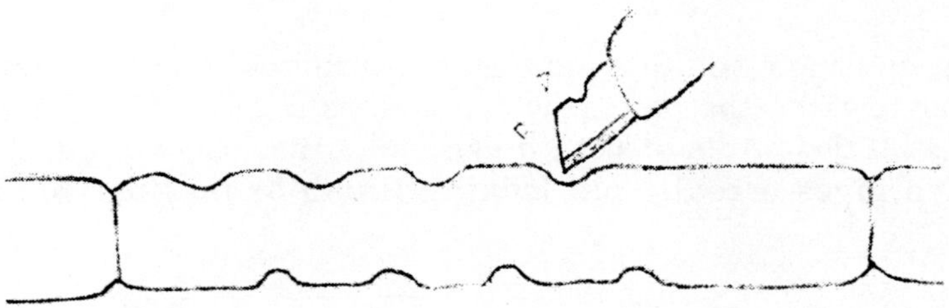

Once that has been done, use your utility knife to cut into the sawed line from either side to form a ridge as above.

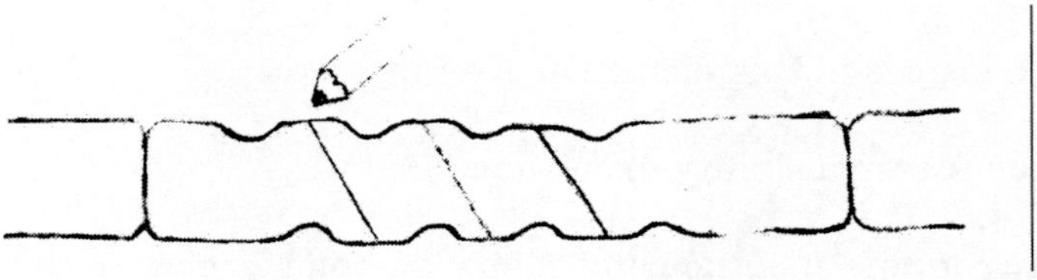

After that, re-do the pencil line in-between the ridges. Use the saw once again but do not saw as deep into the wood this time. When you come to cut the ridge make the ridge a little shallower than the one you did before.

[You can vary the distance between ridges, making them wider towards the bottom which creates a good effect. Sand the staff down to a smooth finish and either use wood stain, which gives a really old looking finish or just use plain

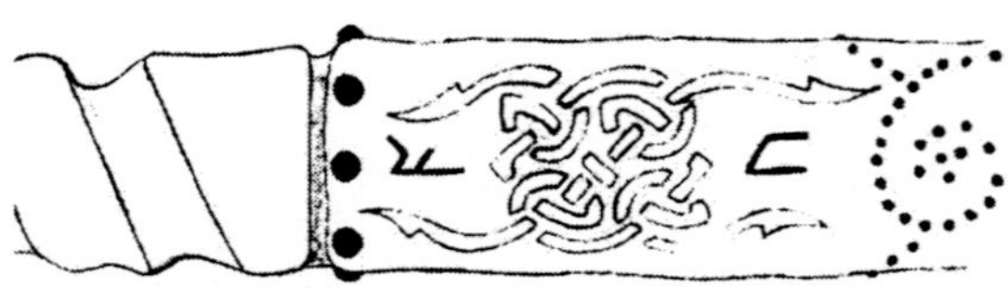

varnish that will enhance the natural wood]

The runes in this picture above represent:

ác : A responsibility to our ancestral ways.

Aurochs: An outpouring of energy, and someone of the craft.]

There are no limitations to your imagination when creating the work of art that shall become your staff. You may choose something plain and simple or opt for a more elaborate object with weaves and spirals inlaid with a multitude of brass studs, whichever design you choose will stand as a symbol of your cunning, the banner that is Lybláс and a beacon of the Anglo Saxon Witch.

Staff brandings

Runes
(runstaef)

In ancient times the most widely used form of runes used by our Wiccan (Witch-ahn) ancestors was the Rune Stave. The rûnstæf as it was then known was a little different to the more widely accepted form of runes used today.

The "staves" were cut from mostly fruit trees with each rune being cut from a different branch. The rune stave would have to be no more than about 7 inches long, usually the measurement would be from tip of the thumb, to the tip of the index finger with both finger and thumb outstretched in an "L" shape ie from tip to tip!

This "L" shape was obviously the laguz rune signifying the strength of water and the ebb and flow of power from the roots of Yggdrasill the world tree. This power being "drawn up" as with any tree that gets sustenance from its roots is the gift that gives the sustenance, magical knowledge and might and power of the web. Although the laguz rune often signifies a downward flow of energy in this instance the force is flowing up from deep within mother earth and the web itself.

The staves should be carved and tapered at one end with the rune of choice being burned or carved into the flat opposite end. More often than not blood was used to give the rune its colour and sense of connection with the Gods, the "rûncwysta" (a rune teller/speaker) would not be failing if instead of blood red pigment such as red ochre was used.

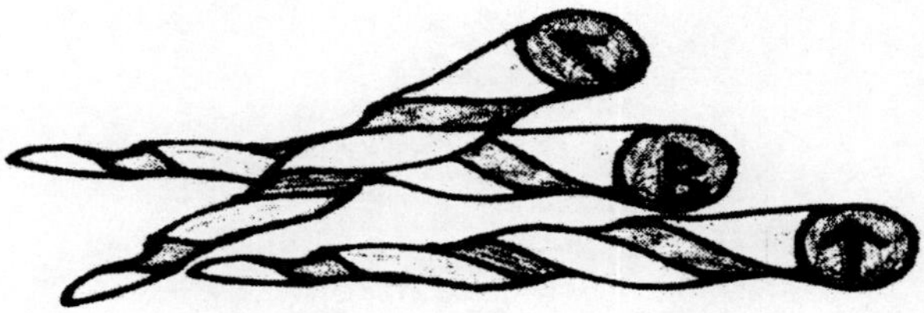

Rune staves can be carved in the same way as a wand but it does not have to be spiralled; they can be plain, tapered and sanded.

Note that as the rune staves are fashioned a low voiced charging song (song of enchantment) should be sung over them to help "wake" the runes to life.

ᚠ

Fehu/Féoh/Fee

Féoh, (Wealth/Money) is No 1 of the 1st "Aett" of the Anglo Saxon Futhorc which consists of 29 + runes as opposed the elder Futhark which has only 24. It corresponds to the English letter "F" and the sound "F" as in "Franks".

Pronounced "Fee" in the middle of words (i.e.; as in offer) the F rune originally meant money and the power over domesticated animals.

Cattle were used as money and barter by our ancestors for all sorts of food, goods and to help sustain their everyday lives. Féoh`s/Fee's power later became transferred to the meanings of Gold, jewellery and eventually coins.

Its Anglo-Saxon rune poem reads:

Fee (Money) a wealth and help --- to every one
Though every man should --- share it out freely
If before the Lord --- a righteous name they should hold.

Féoh/Fee symbolises all that money brings power, standing, possessions, wealth, and as stated in its A.S. rune poem, it embodies mobile power that must be distributed evenly and given freely. As Fee is likened to a double-edged sword, the downfall or shadow part of this rune comes from not having the foresight and wisdom to release the ebb and flow of its fire. If no forethought is given when using this rune it can precipitate a move into greed, envy and strife to which destruction and discord amongst kinsman shall follow. Social and monetary success can be easily won with Féoh/Fee. It can also bring an inner wealth, an all encompassing knowledge and nourishment for the human soul. The origin of this rune's power lies in "well being," and having the cunning not to let its abundance overflow and eventually burn you out.

Key word: Wealth.

On a prophetic level: Féoh means you shall soon be in a position to generate wealth, but downfall will come if one hoards the wealth.

Drýcræft: (Magical workings) Wealth in all its forms.

Light side: Social success, Wealth & energy, Foresight, New beginnings.

Shadow side: Greed, Poverty, "Burnout," Discord, Disharmony.

ᚢ

Ur/Uruz/Aurochs

Ur, (Ox) is the second of the Anglo Saxon Futhorc, and corresponds to the English letters "U" and the sound "u" as in "Bull".

The U rune originally meant the power of the now extinct Urochs. The Aurochs was one of the largest Bovines ever to walk the earth. From its skeletal remains we can see that it was at least 7 feet tall at the shoulder, and a very formidable beast indeed.

Pronounced "OO-RR" like the deep resonating sound of the beast's voice. This "Wild-Ox" of our ancestors was the ultimate principle of vital life forces and boundless energy.

Its Anglo-Saxon rune poem reads:

Aurochs all savage --- and strong horned
A fearsome beast --- that fights with horns
A well-known moor traveller --- the bravest of bold creatures.

Ur symbolises ability, defence, ferocity and vital strength. Its manifestation being the protection of the home and family, and the burning away all weakness and dross (Scum of metals; refuse; rubbish.)

In ancient times the Teutonic tribes would hunt the Aurochs to test the manhood of their warriors. The Germanic tribes heavily prized the horns of this great beast, as drinking vessels, while its meat and hide helped to sustain the people through the hardships of the biting winter.

This rune of determination gives great strength to those needing to accomplish arduous tasks, giving might where it is needed and cunning to evade the wolf.

Key word: Might.

On a prophetic level: Ur denotes that great strength will be needed and the bravery to use it.

Drycræft: (Magical workings) Vigour, strength, Solidity.

Light side: Defence, Unyielding force, Freedom, Strength, Understanding.

Shadow side: Foolishness, Frailty, Weakness, Misdirection, & Ignorance.

ᚦ

Thorn/Thurisaz/Thurs

Thorn, is the third rune of the Futhorc; it corresponds to the English letters "TH" and the sound "Th" as in "Thorn". The Thorn rune is the epitome of shielding energies. In nature, thorns protect plants from too much grazing by beasts and birds alike and so too can this rune be a protector for human kind. As Thurs (The ancient Giants of Norse legend) this rune can be seen as the primitive and primeval force, a preoccupation of obsessive nature that will threaten all order. This rune of Thunor/Thor like the hammer, is a powerful and protective symbol. A rune of silent and reliable defence as anyone who has ever pruned a rose or blackberry bush will know. Thorn dutifully warns all to "Watch out" as it draws blood from the unwary.

Its Anglo-Saxon rune poem reads:

Thorn is painful --- and sharply pricks any person
To court its bite -- you shall reap evil
For all who rest --- amongst them.

Thorn symbolises protective and active energies, a penetrating and mighty weapon against evil, safeguarding kith, kin and property. It also has a somewhat phallic symbolism that relates to the de-flowering and the drawing of blood when capturing a maiden's virginity.

Thorn gives the warning "Never to grasp into the darkness" and also "Once bitten twice shy" and as with both senses above, there is no turning back once the step has been taken.

Key word: Shield.

On a prophetic level: Thorn augurs a time of measured, self-preservation. A time to beware of those who would do harm. Protect yourself.

Drýcræft: (Magical workings) Shielding & defence, also cursing.

Light side: Defence, a guarding force, championing a cause, a shield. Foresight & forethought.

Shadow side: Fear, betrayal, Spite, unapproachable, defenceless.

ᚩ

Òs/Anuz/áss/Ethel

Òs, (God) is the fourth letter of the Futhorc and corresponds to the English letter "A" and the sound "A" as in "Ark". The rune of the Lord Woden and of all that is hidden, Òs is symbolic of wisdom and secrets won through self sacrifice. It is the rune of the "Shaman" and of "Spoken & written Galdor" the "A" rune, also shows the self within the community and his/her interaction there with. Communication, speech and all forms of language are bound up in the complexities of this mighty rune. As our forefathers saw words and the singing thereof as magic, the power of Òs is proven to be inherent in all forms of verbal and written magic and is synonymous with the extraction of energy and power through the forging of such oral and inscribed runic charms or spells.

Its Anglo-Saxon rune poem reads:

> God is the cradle of all language --- the structure of enlightenment
> The profound --- solace of all humankind
> And to every brave person --- plentiful of promise.

Òs symbolises hidden knowledge and the fact that through self-sacrifice godly power and wisdom can be obtained. Our lord Woden himself when hanging from the world tree starved and thirsted as none gave him food nor drink, which eventually and after nine agonising nights led to the secrets of language and that of written galdor being released to him. Thus through his oblation magic and wisdom of the runes was delivered unto humankind.

Key words: Communication.

On a prophetic level: Òs can mean a time of spiritual knowledge. You will hear the right words. Reward for past effort, Opening up.

Drýcræft: (Magical workings) Eloquence, binding & bonding. Influence. Divine aid and knowledge. The truth.

Light side: Knowledge, Integrity, Discovery, The runes, Know how, Esoteric revelations, Openness.

Shadow side: Blinded, Failure to comprehend, Unreasoning, Alienating, Foolish, Hiding.

ᚱ

Ræd/rád/Raidho

Ræd (To ride) is the fifth letter of the Futhorc and corresponds to the English letter "R" and the sound "R" as in "Round". The rune of journeys, riding, and motion it reflects the passage of time in an endless wheel likened to the seasons that are always moving and re-forming in a never ending cycle of life and death. In the Elder Futhark Raidho is seen as the long, and somewhat difficult road of one's own personal growth, showing the order with which change can and will occur.

Its Anglo-Saxon rune poem reads:

Journeying is for --- all warriors
Soft and very active --- for those who sit above
The strong sea --- has many milestones to cross

The sea referred to above, is the exploration and ups and downs of life that we all should undertake, meeting the many uncharted paths on the mysterious road to fulfilment and enlightenment. Of course all seems easy for those who chose to travel a lazy and more simpler route, opting for the shy and timid approach, never taking things head on and missing out on the experiences and true growth that life has to offer. When an evil deed is perpetrated against you, if no reaction to the evildoer is undertaken, then that is, and was, seen as an altogether damaging and unbalanced approach for the individual and for the tribe as a whole. Any ensuing evil force, would lead to a loss of self worth and bad luck if no reciprocating action was embarked upon.

Key word: Exertion.

On a prophetic level: Ræd means motion, a Journey both physically and spiritually. Rewards for past efforts. Reaching a new level of clarity and understanding. Moving up a level.

Drýcræft: (Magical workings) Transportation, Action, Planning, Growth.

Light side: Movement, Journeying, and Reward for hard labours.

Shadow side: Inactivity, Rigidity, Laziness, and Stagnation. Injustice.

<

Cén/Kenaz/Kaunaz

Cén (Torch) is the sixth letter of the Futhorc and corresponds to the English letter "C" and the hard sound "K" as in "Kite" unless doubled "CC" or before "i" & "e" then it is sounded "CH" as in "Witch" (Wicce/Witch-uh).

Our ancestors used fire denoted by the Cén rune to protect and shield all that may need a defence against the evil that is the darkness. This rune of fire and light ensured the banishment of illness and disease, all that passed through the cleansing flames of Cén should reap the blessings of the light. (After parting a fire livestock were driven through the middle so as to rid them of parasites and illness. Bread and Ale were carried through and blessed in the same way.)

Its Anglo-Saxon rune poem reads:

Torch lives --- and is known by all
Shining and brilliant --- burning often
Even where --- the highborn rest

Rune of creation and controlled creativity Cén is a holy beacon lighting our way through the gloom of the unknown. Cleansing and purifying the brilliance of its light and radiance reveal the inspiration of the gods, lighting our way through the shadows destroying all that is unclean and unworthy.

Key word: Design.

On a prophetic level: Cén means health will be an issue, clean living and the curbing of excess are needed. Renewed vigour through inspiration and enlightenment, reshaping and bettering your situation, health.

Drýcræft: (Magical workings) Impetus and ability. Cleansing. Banishment.

Light side: Creation, energy, direction, animation, stimulation, and purity.

Shadow side: Darkness and shadow, misdirection, illness, introversion.

ᚷ

Gifu/Gyfu/Giefu/Gebo

Gifu (Gift) is the seventh letter of the Futhorc and corresponds to the English letters "G & J" and the hard sound "G" as in "Gift" and also a softer "J" sound as in "Gymnasium". Gifu denotes the exchange of ideas, sacrifice, love and magical understanding between not only the gods and man, but also between all those bound in partnerships of any kind. If respect, honour and attention is given then from magical knowledge to the deepest love will be bestowed upon those that seek the way of Gifu. In Anglo Saxon times "The gift" between two separate peoples/tribes was of the utmost importance, from the betrothal of the high born to reparation through gold, silver and land without which, the clans would of never have survived.

Its Anglo-Saxon rune poem reads:

Gifu is the honour song --- of all men
A support and veneration --- to all
A messenger and shelter --- when needs are most

I see Gifu as the rune of Erca the earth goddess. The gift of life and of sustenance comes from her. Without the great mother, nothing would exist. We give nature the gift of nurture tending the fields, feeding and watering the land and in turn she The Mother gives us food, shelter, nourishment and wellbeing. She feeds our livestock with lush pasture and grants the ultimate gifts that help us all to live our lives in harmony through kith, kin and our environment.

Key word: Benefaction.

On a prophetic level: (Magical workings) releasing the gift of wellbeing. Exchange of ideas. What is given should be received. Hospitality.

Drýcræft: To receive gifts. To gain experience. Reciprocation. Material & spiritual endowments. Sustenance. Sacrifice.

Light side: Equality, Power through mutual exchange, Love, Nurture.

Shadow side: Reliance on others, Loss of magical power, Avarice.

ᚹ

Wyn/Wynn/Wunjo

Wyn (Enjoyment) is the eighth letter of the Futhorc and corresponds to the English letter "W" and the sound "W" as in "Win". The Wyn rune is the rune of pleasure and of family harmony, a sort of talisman against sorrows, making the power of positive thought paramount and the principle of its being. Elation and exaltation luck and lust are the order of the day when using the Wynn rune. Needs are met and desires experienced by the last of Freya`s eight, building self-esteem as wishes are won where bliss and happiness are forged.

Its Anglo-Saxon rune poem reads:

Wyn can he never know --- whose sorrows are few
And for him self --- little anguish has
Inspiration is the torch --- as confidence grows dark

Wyn is of living life to the full but at the same time incorporating fellowship and high ideals. It is the knowing how exactly to take the most from all that you now have, safe in the knowledge that the true value lies in knowing a time when comforts were few and hardships built character.

Key word: Magnanimity.

On a prophetic level: Wyn augurs a time of great joy and elation. Harmony. A new relationship. Comradeship. Affability.

Drycræft: (Magical workings) Joy, Brightness, Merriment, Blessedness.

Light side: Enjoyment, Welfare, Happiness, Favourability, Luck and Lust.

Shadow side: Sadness and sorrow, Strife, Alienation, Conflict, Struggle.

ᚻ

Hægl/Hagol/Hagalaz

Hagol (Hail) is the ninth letter of the Futhorc and corresponds to the English letter "H" and the sound "H" as in "hail". Hægl starts the second "Aett" or octet of the Anglo Saxon Alphabet and has aspects of transition, as ice turns to water, and being a double-edged rune loaded with aspects of destruction that also align with nourishment and life as the water giver. Hagol is a rune of the god Woden and of winter where everything sleeps giving time to heal and prepare for the oncoming seasons.

Its Anglo-Saxon rune poem reads:

Hail song --- the whitest corn
Of heaven's breath --- it tumbles
It billows from the wind --- it is made water afterwards

The principle of being cruel to be kind is an aspect of this rune, the A.S. rune poem above states that Hail, which can be harsh and destructive is also seen as White Corn or Grain.

From a sudden and dangerous storm comes the water's of creation, as the hail transforms the land as it melts away disappearing into the earth nourishing the flora and fauna, refreshing mother earth. So we can note that the Hagol rune is very much a rune of transformation. It also shows us that not everything is as it seems. But for the most part it creates something good from something first seen as bad and that life, like the harshness of the hard winter can and will inevitably give way to the abundance and new growth of the oncoming season of spring.

Key word: Metamorphosis.

On a prophetic level: Hagol foretells a time of short-lived upheaval. That every cloud can have a silver lining. To look beyond the immediate.

Drýcræft: (Magical workings) Fertility, Creation, Short lived anguish.
A turnaround.

Light side: Potential through hard work. Natural cycles, Change, Regulated crisis.

Shadow side: Loss of power, Disaster, Break down, Obstruction.

ᚾ

Nýd/Níed/Nauthiz

Nýd is the tenth letter of the Futhorc and corresponds to the English letter "N" and the sound "N" as in "Need." The rune of want and necessities proves that for humankind to "need" is something not necessarily bad or undesirable. As its rune poem below suggests; Nýd pushes all forward into the realms of creation both on a spiritual and mental level, delivering us from stagnation and our inherent sense of holding back. Thus Nýd inspires us to use whatever gifts we have, to resist the shackles of restraint forming and establishing self-reliance in the creation of original fire through humankind's problem solving and of "thought" itself.

Its Anglo-Saxon rune poem reads:

Need is a distress --- on the minds of men
Yet frequently in his offspring --- a help and safety
If they rather listen --- to themselves

Nýd represents the lessons learned within the trials and tribulations of our earthly existence. The overcoming of strife in our daily endeavours which leads to the eternal contest of mind over matter and the reasoning of humankind to turn around stress from a negative into a positive.

Key word: Necessity.

On a prophetic level: Foretells a time of strife and conflict, hindrance, blockage. Great reliance on ones self is needed.

Drýcræft: (Magical workings) Nýd can be used to overcome or increase the above.

Light side: Control through contemplation. Turn around for the good. Might through impedance.

Shadow side: Distress, Contention, Hostility, Hindrance, Feelings of defeat.

ᛁ

Is/îzas/Isa

Is (Ice) is the eleventh letter of the Futhorc and corresponds to the English letter "I" and the sound "i" as in "bid." The rune of caution Is shows us that we should "never judge a book by its cover". A prognostic sign Is summons man's will to make sure of the facts before embarking on any endeavour. It gives a stark warning for us to be aware of those who would deceive us.

The beauty of ice belies its power, a force so great that it can stop the Sea, crack solid rock and literally "move mountains", it is the opposite force of Sigil (the rune of fire) in which it is eternally combined in the overture that is creation, giving form to our very existence but also summoning caution as all can be wiped out faster than a blink of a eye.

Its Anglo-Saxon rune poem reads:

Ice is beyond cold --- and immeasurably perilous
Glistening transparent --- a jewels likeness
Ground wrought of frost --- an object of favour

Beautiful and precious, steadfast and deleterious the rune of ice is attractive and enticing but an altogether unforgiving master that can freeze the ego and bring all to a crushing standstill. It teaches us to always look beyond first impressions, and that maybe there is a light within the darkness and that the bridge between in-action and action is change itself.

Key word: Caution.

On a prophetic level: Be careful all is not as it seems

Drycræft: (Magical workings) Is can be used to force a halt to something. Also to "Turn the lights on" so to speak in a realisation of the truth.

Light side: Waking up, Comprehension and an acquisition of knowledge, Attraction. Beauty.

Shadow side: Darkness, Immovability, Frozen, and the over ego, Stress.

ᛄ

Géar/Jera /ár/Gér

Géar (Year) is the twelfth letter of the Futhorc and corresponds to the English letter "G/J" and the sound "Y" as in "year". Géar is the rune of sowing and of reaping, whether it is on a physical or spiritual level "Year" symbolises the period of time between the two points.

This rune of hope lies midway between man and his efforts to bring together those elements that will result in growth. Like the clearing of the ground so that the sun can warm the fields and the watering and feeding of the crops to bring forth a promised bounty. Géar tells us that whatever you put in we get out, and from the smallest of seed nurtured and tended will reward us greatly.

Its Anglo-Saxon rune poem reads:

Géar is to all humankind --- a comfort thereon if god allows
Holy king of heaven --- a gift of the earth if she wills
Blossoming fruit --- for rich and poor alike

Géar measures spring, summer and the harvest, the natural cycle of the year which is opposite to the harshness of the dark and cleansing of winter. Its power lies within its ruling of that time, a time of peace and reward that can bring productivity, affluence, fruitfulness and wealth.

Key word: Comfort.

On a prophetic level: Reward, Rebirth, and Fruition.

Drýcræft: (Magical workings) claiming what is owed.

Light side: Fruitfulness, Benefit, Interest, and Yield, Harvest.

Shadow side: Redundancy, ill timed, unproductive, Loss.

ᛇ

Éoh/Eihwaz/Yew

Éoh (Yew) is the thirteenth letter of the Futhorc and corresponds to the English letters "ih" and the sound "æ" as in "had/has". The mark of protection and the rune of magic Éoh connects the sky and the earth emulating the great world tree that brings the light of the sun into the darkness and belly of the mother. The Yew is the brightest of trees in the dark, long winter. It spits stars (sparks) when burned and holds the strength of the bow. Symbolically existing in the "Middle World" between life and death Éoh symbolises humankind's journey from ungodly creatures to the realisation of our other/spiritual natures.

Its Anglo-Saxon rune poem reads:

Yew on the outside --- is uneven and rough
Firm rooted --- steadfast and fires form
A support and foundation --- blithe on native soil

Very strong with a red core the Yew was fashioned into runes and very long staves that would come to represent the magical staffs of office for the Lyblæca/Lybbestre. This rune shows how in the depths of winter when all seems barren and dead, the spirit of life still holds on. It shows that although on the outside all seems grim, dark and lifeless, that inside there still burns the fire and the vivacity of human existence.

Key word: Illumination.

On a prophetic level: You will have to defend yourself. A conclusion.

Drycræft: (Magical workings) Enhancement of power, Life and death.

Light side: Deep knowledge, Rune magic, Connection between the worlds, The ancestors.

Shadow side: Death, Banishment, Curses, and Termination. Chaos.

(Warning: The Yew is very toxic and a hallucinogen)

ᛈ

Peorth/Perþ/oerp/perthro

Peorth (Chessmen?) is the fourteenth letter of the Futhorc and corresponds to the English letter "P" and the sound "P" as in "Pour". This mighty rune gives supreme confidence and knowledge of impending success in battle. Fearlessly its fortune is also bound up with the act of "Ale drinking" and games of chance. The chancing of one's arm was a great passion and a way of life for the northern European tribes. Ale was seen as a magical draught, the reason for this is not very hard to see as after just a few tankards of ealoð/ealu, "Boldness" and "Nerve" became quickly evident.

Peorth conjures up the familiar picture of Saxon and Viking times, where ale halls full of loud and fearless warriors downed tankards in one gulp and played games of chance.

Its Anglo-Saxon rune poem reads:

Peorth is forever a drama --- and the laughter of boastful men
As they sit --- and make war
Together in the Ale hall --- united under the sun

A rune of fellowship and of the firing up of one's soul the Peorth rune brings tribesmen and kin together in a bonding of hearts, minds and souls.

A rune of evolution, strength and cunning for individual and clan alike, it sends forth a stout-hearted resolve when meeting seemingly overwhelming forces head on and even holds fast the very fear of death itself.

Key word: Fearlessness.

On a prophetic level: A time of get together and of bonding, family events. Love and laughter

Drýcræft: (Magical workings) For daring and fortitude. Meeting one's fate.

Light side: Good company, Kinship, life and laughter. Acceptance, Boldness,
Having no fear.

Shadow side: Being bad looser, Bitterness, Going too far, Alcoholism.

ᛉ

Algiz/Eolh/ Eolhsecg/Elhaz

Eolh (Elk) Eolhsecg (reed) is the fifteenth letter of the Futhorc and corresponds to the very early English letter "Z/S" and the sound Z/S in "bows". The ultimate rune of protection Eolh has the talismanic power of Deity, and of sacred and holy places. Unlike Thorn Eolh does not shield through an attacking force drawing blood in the process, the "Z" rune brings the wrath of the gods and of spirit to bear when unitising its safeguarding and securing powers. Eolh also gives a way in which humankind can reach deity, but in doing so warns us all of the pitfalls and concealed dangers if we are unprepared or unworthy for such an overwhelming and magnificent journey.

Its Anglo-Saxon rune poem reads:

Elk-reed holds native soil --- enduring in the marshes
From beneath water it grows --- wounding cruelly
Burns the blood --- of all that would wish to of take it

As the Lyblæca/Lybbestre stand before the altar in the Algiz position, in doing so it serves to invoke godly protection not only for the sacred space or Spirit grove (gastbearu) but insuring that all unwanted or baneful energies are kept at bay from everyone that within it.

Key words: The wrath of the gods.

On a prophetic level: The gods will protect you if you

prepare yourself for what is to come.

Dryċræft: (Magical workings) Asking for, and obtaining the protection of the gods. The realisation that "They" will act on your behalf.

Light side: Knowledge and divine acceptation. A safe harbour. Guardianship, protector.

Shadow side: Calamity and destruction if one is not prepared or worthy.

ᛋ

Sigel/Sigil/Sówuló/Sól

Sigel (Sun) is the sixteenth letter of the Futhorc and corresponds to the English letter "S" and the sound "S" as in "Sky". As the rune of the sun and of the sky Sigel lends a feminine and nurturing touch to the aspect of the northern European summer. Through its fervency and radiating power Sigel is associated with Sól/Sunné the sun goddess and her journey across the heavens. The "S" rune has a very emphatic and positive countenance, which brings forth light, heat, and favour upon the land and its peoples. The opposite of Ice, this rune of fire is also associated with "brynebeorg" the Fire Mountains of the south and also connects to the earth mother as she gives birth to the world.

Its Anglo-Saxon rune poem reads:

Sun is a never-ending desire --- when seamen ride the fish's bath
Until such a time -- that No-bridel should bring them to land

Banishing the darkness that we all must enter, Sigel teaches us to search for veracity, foresight and knowledge. The path of the sun rune leads us to seek enlightenment and the higher self, and ever in motion the sun wheel awakens the soul as feelings of well being and life emanate from its golden rays, filling us with hope, anticipation and eagerness for a lucky and favourable journey ahead.

Key word: Expectation

On a prophetic level: A time of security and contentment. A favourable voyage/trip.

Drýcræft: (Magical workings) For ensuring a reliable outcome. An auspicious and a favourable journey. Safety. Fortune.

Light side: Hope, Confidence, Trust, Belief, Warmth, and Nurturing, Luck. Safe journey.

Shadow side: Depression, Being crushed, Despondency, and Helplessness. A disastrous excursion/trip.

ᛏ

Tir/T√ r/Tiw/Teiwaz/Tiwaz

Tir (Honour/fame) is the seventeenth letter of the Futhorc and the start of the third Eight, corresponding to the English letter "T" and the sound "T" as in "Title". The "T" rune is associated with loyalty, allegiances and oaths between warriors and kin alike.

The rune of Tý r, the northern god of war is where we get the name Tuesday (Tiwesdaeg) from and its symbol was used as a magical charm for conquest. Tir prepares the way after just examination for the bounty and spoils of triumph that can be bestowed upon the righteous and is seen as holding the very essence of fairness and equity.

Tir (The North Star) sets the standard and criteria that shall determine the worthiness and truth of any expected victory. It should also be noted that those who seek the power of Tir should gain discernment only through self-sacrifice. An example being the lord Woden plucking out an eye for the runes whilst hanging from the world tree.

Its Anglo-Saxon rune poem reads:

Tìr shall be a symbol of the many --- which holds truth well
All highborn --- ever on the journey to old age
Overhead the night's darkness --- gives no doubt

Tir will favour those who have forged distinguished and noble lives. All of our past deeds and actions shall be judged as we court divine justice.

Key word: Conquest

On a prophetic level: A time of realisation. A true friend. You will hold all the cards.

Drýcræft: (Magical workings) justness. Favourable court & legal proceedings. Omnipotent & godly rulings. Winning.

Light side: Truth and justice. Recognition. Enlightenment. Self sacrifice for a higher purpose.

Shadow side: Undisciplined. Disappointment. The jaws of the wolf. Immolation.

ᛒ

Beorc/Berkano/Berkana/Barch

Beorc (Birch) is the eighteenth letter of the Futhorc. The B rune corresponds to the English letter "B" and the sound "b" as in "Birth".

The enigma of Beorc is illuminated in mystery of birth and re-birth, and must therefore be associated with the great mother. A rune of life and of prolific productivity Beorc is the talisman for creation and bloodline through birth itself, without ever actually being born.

Beorc also has the connection of the Birch goddess Freya who as it is said took on many of her mother's attributes being the champion of women and of childbirth.

Its Anglo-Saxon rune poem reads:

Birch is without crop --- but nevertheless blossoms
Branches outside shooting --- radiant in there beauty
Proud it adorns the helm --- justly leaf laden it presses the sky

The B rune teaches us to deliver any concealed or latent force, letting it burst forth upon the world, thus ushering in a dawning of new and renewed growth and productivity. The womb of invention, Beorc acts like a harbouring cocoon that helps make ideas and life itself metamorphose and transform from the ethereal and realm of the mind into the physical, here and now.

Key word: Birth, re-birth

On a prophetic level: Beorc augurs a time of transformation and beauty. A blossoming.

Drýcræft: (Magical workings) making manifest that which is within. Protection.

Light side: Birth and conception, Growth, Motherly love, Lineage, Progeny, Creation, Protection, A harbour, Countenance.

Shadow side: Misdirection, No support, Disapproval, Deceitful, Illusory, Dormancy, Decay.

ᛖ

Eh/Ehwaz/Ehwo/Eoh

Eh (Horse/Steed) is the nineteenth letter of the Futhorc and corresponds to the English letter "E" and the sound "E" as in "Led". Used amongst other things by the northern tribes of Europe for divinatory purposes the Horse rune was also extensively used in potent fertility charms. It is said that the "E" rune represents the stance and legs of a horse, bringing into being forces of credibility, faithfulness and the pure essence of trust between man and beast. Ehwaz in its horse form was very often carved on stone and metal, showing and projecting a positive and protective form of Magical power/ Galdor.

Its Anglo-Saxon rune poem reads:

Eh is before Earls -- and high born a joy
Fighters mark --- stately horses hooves
Rich on war steeds --- that are bartered for
Forever a consolation --- to the un-resting

A rune of movement and of conveyance its collaborative and synergetic properties show us the delight, joy and enhancing effects, that can be gained from working together, pertaining to all enlightened partnerships and the benefits that will be received by all concerned.

Key word: Teamwork.

On a prophetic level: Augurs a time of marriage/ partnerships. Loyalty and co-operation.

Drycræft: (Magical workings) Collaboration and assistance.

Light side: Unity, Harmony, Aid, Motion, Allies, Connection, and Protection.

Shadow side: Seduction, Mistrust, Violation, Isolation, Delusion.

ᛗ

Man/Mannaz/Madhr

Man (Humankind) is the twentieth letter of the Futhorc and corresponds to the English letter M" and the sound "M" as in "Man".

The Mannaz rune shows both sides of humankind's primal essence, from its strengths to its frailty, from the ups and downs of everyday existence to loyalties and the road that leads to betrayal. The power of the M rune reveals everything, warts and all, and in doing so shows us the possibilities and potential that we as people can be or become when being totally open to ourselves and the truth.

In knowing and using the M rune, we find that through experience and openness our earthly and heavenly lives can lead to a better understanding and also to the realisation of our own and humankind's potential, vivacity, weakness and mortality.

Its Anglo-Saxon rune poem reads:

Man is a joyous sound --- beloved of kinsmen
Yet all shall be found wanting -- the doom of mankind
God's wishes shall take the poor flesh -- the earth to give

A rune of insight and connection Man reveals our true worth and our kinship to the gods. It should however be noted that in doing so Man also reveals our own survival instincts, when the chips are down it can denote a time when our noble virtues fail us. We seek to preserve our own identity and lives, even when those that we hold so dear can be betrayed or even destroyed in the process.

Key word: Reality.

On a prophetic level: Can augur a time of revelation, also one should beware of possible betrayal.

Drȳcræft: (Magical workings) Illumination, Knowing one's limitations.

Light side: Insight, Life, Understanding, Self-preservation, and godly connection, Humanity.

Shadow side: Mortality, Betrayal, Over self-preservation, Callousness, corruption, uncaring.

ᛚ

Lagu/Laguz/Leac/Laukaz/Logr.

Lagu (Ocean/great-water/Body of water) is the twenty-first letter of the Futhorc and corresponds to the English letter "L" and the sound "L" as in "Lake".

A journey rune belonging to the great Thunor god of thunder, the L rune's wild and storm-torn aspects are felt from within the journey of all life that all must undertake. Sudden and unexpected events can erupt from beneath the calm of an unprepared existence but should we choose to control the rapid and explosive fire of these aspects, greatness and success will surly be ours for the taking. The message of Laguz is that the hardships and testing situations that arise out of the blue can be overcome with the right preparations, giving us control over that which many let devastate them giving us the upper hand over whatever is thrown our way.

Its Anglo-Saxon rune poem reads:

Water appears without end --- to all humanity
If on an unsteady vessel --- he should ride
The mighty sea waves shall him --- severely terrify
When the sea stallion --- no bridal respects

A rune of initiation of birth and of the last journey that we all must take at the time of death Laguz can be seen as the deluge or cataclysmic upheaval resulting from our inability to look before we leap. A cycle of cause and effect resulting from our past acts and deeds, the fact being, if we do not properly prepare for the journey ahead then the fault must be from within ourselves when things go wrong. These waters of life show that we travel through water to get here and indeed travel across water to get the realms of the dead when we depart, with the in-between being the ebb and flow of our journey to enlightenment. Riding the waves when secure in the knowledge that you are well prepared gives rapid growth and great reward.

Key word: Fluidity.

On a prophetic level: Can augur a time of prolific and swift change.

Drýcræft: (Magical workings) The controlling of unseen forces, for good or bad.

Light side: Fluidity, Growth, Journeying, Rapid healing, Animation, Vigour.

Shadow side: All encompassing fear and blinded to change, Devastation & destruction, Rapid decay.

ᛝ

Ing/Ingwaz/Inguz

Ing (Hero) is the twenty-second letter of the Futhorc and corresponds to the English letters "NG" and the sound "ng" as in "spring". Rune of the fertility god Ingui Fréa, Ing brings abundance, frith and times of exuberance to those who keep peace and honour with kith and kin. Inguz, the original English green man is consort to the mother goddess Nerthus and tentatively courts her love and affections. This in turn overflows spreading unforeseen benefaction to all from this most virile of gods. In the cult of the great mother those priests who attended her and performed sacred duties took their names directly from her champion Ingui Fréa, I myself am known as Ingár Wulfeage within that Priesthood.

Its Anglo-Saxon rune poem reads:

Ing was first amongst the Danes --- thereafter seen seeking her favour
Beyond went he ---the wagon followed by harsh rain
Thus bold men --- thereafter called him hero

Champion to all, especially when all hope is lost, the god Ing can appear out of the blue to rescue those in need. We all know the story of the shining hero king Arthur who is said to waken from his sleep at a time of great need for England; this is once more a personification of the god Ing who brings all together in peace and kinship.

The rune itself when turned 45 degrees left/right is seen as the symbolic coupling of man and woman when entwined in the act of making love.

Key word: Virility

On a prophetic level: Augurs a time of sudden good fortune.

Drýcræft: (Magical workings) Virility, Vitality, Conception, Peace, Love, Kinship.

Light side: Sex, virility, Potency, Peace, Love, Abundance, Togetherness. Saviour

Shadow side: Impotence, Frailty, Powerlessness, Incapacity, and Sterility.

ᛞ

Dæg/Dagaz/Ðagaz/Dagr

Dæg (Day/Radiance) is the twenty-third letter of the Futhorc and corresponds to the English letter "D" and the sound "D" as in "Day". The D rune corresponds to the emergence of light from within the darkness, like the mighty sun that burns away the gloom, it fills the world with its radiance furnishing the hearts of humankind with joy and delectation.

The rune of enlightenment Dæg, gives us the boost and inspiration that can move us to greet the dawning of new ideas with renewed impetus and vigour helping us to forge ahead with our thoughts and wishes and thus bring them to fruition. The power of Dæg is at its highest at those most magical of times - dawn and dusk.

Its Anglo-Saxon rune poem reads:

Dæg is of god --- beloved of humankind
Splendid creator --- illuminating mirth and desire
That the blessed and poor --- alike shall profit

As the light of day peaks above the horizon we are filled with a sense of optimism and hope, seeking to move ahead spurred on by the realisation that any inaction could result in hopelessness and boredom. When the daylight starts to fade we feel a sense of acceptance and retreat, knowing that we should wait until the time is right, and that if we wish to move forward we should at least "think things through" before any hastiness or rash activity is undertaken.

Key word: Enlightenment.

On a prophetic level: Augurs time of things working out when you stop and think. A light going on. A brand new day. A bright future.

Drycræft: (Magical workings) To create a sunny disposition. To gain intuition and contentment. Also realisation.

Light side: Light, Happiness, Trust, Hope, Sanguinity, and Anticipation, Promise.

Shadow side: Darkness, Rash behaviour, Blindness, Depression, Hopelessness.

ᛟ

Èþel /Othala/éthel

Èþel (Homeland) is the twenty-fourth letter of the Futhorc and corresponds to the English letter "O" and the sound "O" as in "Other". Èþel symbolises true freedom through a firm family base, and the thriving of one's self and one's family. Èþel is symbolic of knowing that through the holding together of the clan that the nurture of magical, spiritual and material values will enhance any family unit so it will grow ever stronger giving greater power to those within. It shows that we are in tune with our past and the ancestors alike and that we are ready to take on the future through strength and power.

Its Anglo-Saxon rune poem reads:

Homeland is beyond love --- for all humankind
Though he is ripped there from --- should he not honour it
And no more enjoy --- the wealth of that household.

The "O" rune is the power within the tribe/clan/family that helps it grow and prosper, and like the circle itself it has no beginning and no end. The legacy that is the Èþel rune of inheritance helps hold society's moral and protective laws well. Binding together the family and tribal unit it gives a sense of history and of wealth that can only be passed on and received through the adherence to appropriate behaviour. If we do not respect our ancestors and the path that has been trodden by our kin to get to this point in time then our true freedom can never be attained. It is only through our heritage and customs and the learning from any mistakes that the whole of society can increase its value.

Key word: Belonging.

On a prophetic level: Augurs a time when things will happen around your Ancestral home, Residence, Property, Native land.

Drýcræft: (Magical workings) Moving home, Adopting a new life and homeland. Bringing the family together.

Light side: A new home, peace through loyalty, prosperity and flouring of the family, magic, Inheritance.

Shadow side: Homelessness, Abandonment and the breakdown of order, loneliness, Self-centredness.

Supplemental A. S. runes:

ᚪ

Ác (Oak)

The 25th rune. Phonetic worth (A)

Its Anglo-Saxon rune poem reads:

> Ác is on earth --- for the offspring of humankind
> Flesh and food it fares --- over the sea birds bath
> The ocean tests --- the Oak's noble truth

As in olden times the mighty Oak was used to build sturdy seafaring ships, its fruit was also used as food for man and beast alike, making it a revered and welcomed part of their everyday existence. Imbued with magical and mystical powers the Oak served as a source of nourishment, strength and enchanting power.

Key word: Strength.

On a prophetic level: A time of needing a strong basis and footing.

Drýcræft: (Magical workings) Empowerment, Might and main. Strength.

Light side: Ability, Efficacy, Stamina, Grit, Force and virtue.

Shadow side: Testing ordeals, Examination, Incapability, Weakness Failing.

ᚫ

Æsc (Ash)

The 26th rune. Phonetic worth (æ)

Its Anglo-Saxon rune poem reads:

Ash is very high --- and to the noble dear
Hard based --- this stallion deserves a strong grasp
Nevertheless he fights --- with (together) all humankind

Ash is the unyielding stance with mighty roots that run deep into the earth, a steadfast anchor when the winds of change blow hard. The wood of the Ash grows relatively straight and so was utilised by our forebears in the construction of spears and similar weaponry and like the world tree Yggdrasil, the Ash connects the worlds especially that of the Lower World and realm of the earth mother.

Key word: Steadfast

On a prophetic level: A time of needing a strong basis and footing.

Drýcræft: (Magical workings) Empowerment, Might and main. Strength and Prediction.

Light side: Ability, Efficacy, and Keeper of the lore, Stamina, Grit, Force and virtue. Prophecy.

Shadow side: Testing ordeals, Examination, Incapability, Weakness Failing.

ᚣ

Yr (Unknown)

The 27th rune.

Its Anglo-Saxon rune poem reads:

> Yew is for highborn and Eorl alike --- a benefaction
> On a horse a fair esteem -- a joy to behold
> Trusted war-gear --- on any road

Yew is the rune of defence and of self-appreciation, it also has a connection with Ash as both are seen as being the world tree and the bridge between the worlds hence Yew being used to contact the ancestors. It is also said that if you meditate beneath a Yew, the tree spirit will proffer prophetic visions to you.

Key word: Value.

On a prophetic level: Augurs a time of blossoming self worth. Pleasures in knowing ones own worthiness. Questions will be answered.

Drýcræft: (Magical workings) Use for maintaining ones standing. And to fortify one's position. Divination.

Light side: Safeguarding, Defence, Exemplary nature, righteousness, Shielding, and Virtue. Integrity. Prediction and Prophesy, Self-acceptance.
Shadow side: Doubt, Hesitation, Mistrust, Vacillation, Undeserving, Defenceless, Unknowing.

ᛡ

Ior (Beaver)

The 28th rune. Phonetic worth (io)

Its Anglo-Saxon rune poem reads:

Ior is the River fish --- which eats on the land
His lodge a fine home --- where happily he abides beset by water

Clouded in the mists of time this rune of "home sweet home" is a somewhat vague contender for the attributes of homely happiness. One would have thought that as it has such a good character that more would have been written about this rune and most precious of states. Related in shape to the Norse rune hagall which is more a rune of new beginnings, from a somewhat violent action Ior also combines protective action conserving and promoting the banishment of inharmonious or negative forces that would upset the delicate balance of the contented home.

Key word: Contentment.

On a prophetic level: Augurs a time of satisfaction and delight.

Drýcræft: (Magical workings) Use for peace and happiness.

Light side: Comfort, Enjoyment, pleasure and reward.

Shadow side: Isolation, Antisocial. Contention, Lacking the bare essentials for a harmonious life.

ᛠ

Ear (Ground/Earth/Grave)

The 29th rune. Phonetic worth (Ea)

Its Anglo-Saxon rune poem reads:

Earth is hideous --- to all fighting men
When heavy flesh starts to grow cold --- in her grasp
Dark prayers from --- dressings of the fallen fruit
Joy is withdrawn --- promise snared

Ear is related to the earth mother Erce and the God Eor/Iar and the Irimsul, indeed when the priests of Nerthus drew her effigy around the villages no weapons were allowed whatsoever as "She" would be angered. When war takes the lives of warriors, indeed they are mourned upon the field of battle and as distressed kin try many times in vain to dress the wounds of the fallen, their soulful distresses hang upon the wind as the lives of loved ones are lost despite the tears that fall upon bloodstained ground. Everything seems to fail but through the fear of what will become of the souls of the slain it becomes apparent that the Ea rune shows us of our own mortality, laying bare our deeds as we realize that all must enter and be consumed one day by the black earth where our deeds will be measured.

Key word: Mortality.

On a prophetic level: Suffering, Illness, and a definite end.

Drýcræft: (Magical workings) Ethically none.

Light side: An end to suffering.

Shadow side: Death.

Rune Spreads

Taking the rune staves from their bag and placing them into the ground.

North Star spread

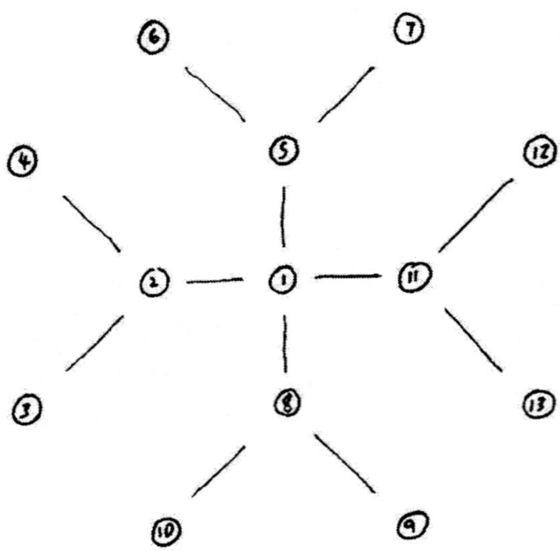

1. Self
2. What has brought you to this point
3. Good experiences

4. Bad experiences
5. Dominating factors
6. Force for good
7. Omens that should have been heeded
8. Underlying decisions & understanding
9. Wrong decisions
10. Wright decisions
11. Course of action - outcome
12. Out-come if action is taken
13. Out-come if action is not taken

As it is known, multiples of 3 were of mystical importance to the Anglo-Saxon and Celtic peoples alike, and as we can see from the above North Star spread the numbers 2+3+4 = 9 which is a multiple of 3 as is 5+6+7, = 18 = 9 and also, 8+9 +10 = 27 = 9 positions and also the 11+12.+13 = 36 = 9. The inner squares of 1+2+5+8+11= 27 = 9 with the north, east, south & west all adding up to the number 3.

Hammer spread

As with the North Star the Hammer spread has its multiples of 3. The hammer itself adding up to 3 and the shaft to 9 with them both together adding up to 21 which equals 3.

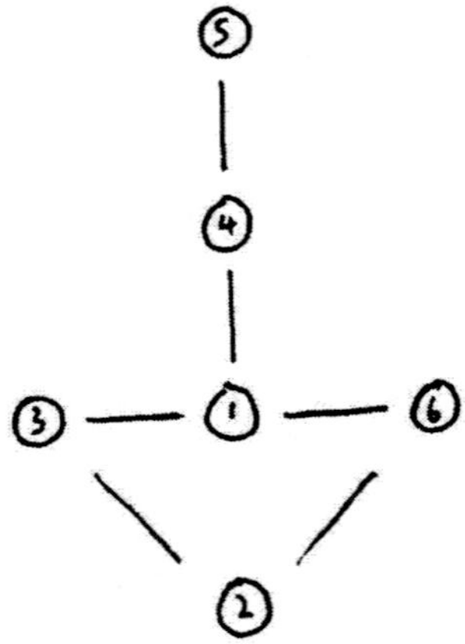

1. Self
2. Problem
3. How you perceive things
4. How others see you
5. Course of action
6. Solution

The Past, Present and future spread below at first seems to buck the trend but on closer inspection the multiples are there. 2 + 1+3 = 6 now 4 + 1+ 2 = 7 & 3 + 4 + 1 = 8 together 6 + 7 + 8 = 21 which in turn is 3. If you take the outer triangles and add 2 + 3 = 5 then 2 + 4 = 6 then 3 + 4 = 7 that makes 5 + 6 + 7 = 18 which in turn makes 9.

Past, Present & Future spread

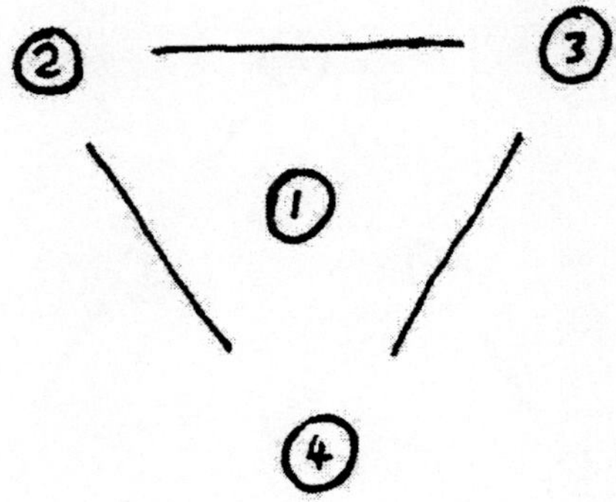

1. Self
2. Past
3. Present
4. Future

Goddess reading

(Love)

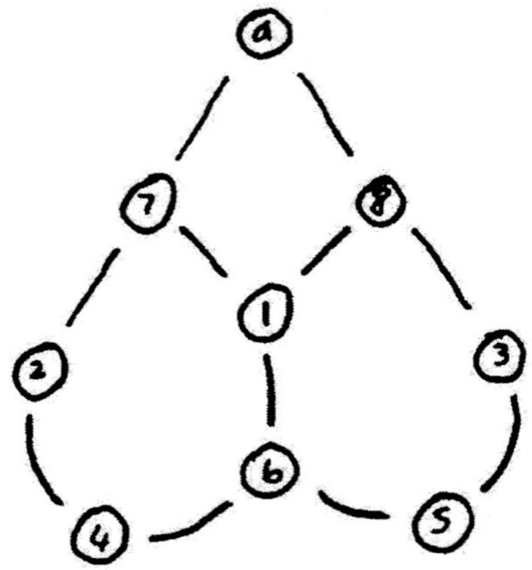

1. Self
2. Situation you find yourself in
3. Situation you would like to be in
4. Past experiences
5. Mistakes made
6. Lessons learned
7. Hopes, Fears

The upside down heart shape of the Goddess stave placement is a very ancient symbol of the Goddess. It represents the bosom and buttocks of the female form, which eventually became inverted, and the familiar heart shape of today.

The number 3 as a special significance where the Goddess is concerned, but as you will notice the three sections in fact make up the number 8 which as we know is the symbol of the never ending knot, the position of the bride and groom's hands as they are handfasted. The three sets of three numbers (lower, middle and upper) all add up to 6 this equates to 3 x 6= 18 and 1+8 = 9

Reading the Runes

The rune reader shall have all the runes concealed within a bag (ideally animal skin), if you wish, fake fur could be substituted. The reading should always be done outdoors on a flat piece of grass or earth with the rune reader sitting opposite the recipient reading with eyes closed (until the runes are revealed) and the right hand deep within the bag. The rune staves are to be moved around by the reader within the bag, as he/she does so the roots of the world tree are envisaged within his/her mind. The rune reader calls:

"Lords and ladies
bestow the right
reveal the web
declare rune might
lift the Veil
o fates unfold
of doors unlocked
and spirit bold"

áwréon
áberan
whliteseon

* áwréon REVEAL *áberan DISCOVER. *whliteseon SIGHT.

The rune staves are then pushed into the earth (just enough to make them stand) starting with the self-position rune.

If the rune staves are made as above making it is easy to push them into the earth and place whatever object/offering to be blessed or empowered on top.

The stave can be carved from a single branch with the length of the stave determined by the distance between the tip of your forefinger and the tip of the thumb. This is symbolic of the Laguz rune with knowledge being drawn up through the roots of the tree from the depths of the earth.

Numbered positions:

1 an.......................11. endleofon
2 twegan................12. twelf
3 thrie....................13. threotiene
4 feower.................14. feowertiene
5 fif.........................15. fiftiene
6 siex......................16. siextiene
7 seofon.................17. seofontiene
8 eaht.....................18. eatiene
9 nigon...................19. nigontiene
10 tien......................20. twentig

Ercen Oracle

(The Water, the wood and the word)

Calling upon the earth mother to give divine guidance can be a very rewarding experience indeed. Such actions help us to nurture an emerging nexus and bonding relationship that will enable the great earth mother herself to guard and guide us always. The Ercen oracle acts upon the principle that the roots of the world tree draw up sustaining waters, giving life and nourishment to the tree. In this way the words and advice of the great mother travel up through the earth, roots and wood revealing themselves unto us in order to nourish and communicate answers to the questioner's quest for truth and knowledge.

What will I need?

A brook/stream/pond.

An earthenware bowl/vessel

Nine flat wooden rune staves.

Nine Ash/Yew twigs (About 12 inches in length) bound together with red cord

Firstly you will have to find a natural stream, brook or pool where you are going to be undisturbed. Taking a largish earthenware bowl place it underneath the water so as to fill it but, letting the water flow freely into and out of the vessel, a few times before filling it to the brim. As you do so recite:

Great Erce, You who were, are and always will be, mother of all humankind
Hear me now.
I am the seeker, at the gates of your wisdom
I pray let your guidance flow through the waters of life
I beseech you mother reveal unto me your secrets
That I may know your honest judgement

Remove the now filled bowl/vessel from the water and place it steadily upon bare soil. Now taking nine pre-selected runes (Chosen whilst you were blindfolded prior from their bag) and holding them in your right hand plunge your left hand into the water and hold the right hand on high. Now as you recite the following words envisage the water travelling from your fingers (Roots) up through your body (The tree) and into the runes (The fruit) that you hold in your right hand.

Say:

Truth is based upon solid foundations
The roots shall hold fast against the howling winds
Life flows rich and steadily upward
The leaves loaded questions of mankind's dreams.
The fruit thereof, is forged of her lore
Reason and right petitioned in meekness

A son / daughter of the great mother
Loyal in virtue
Sing me your song
Mother most wise.

After you have said the above verse, take your left hand from the water and drop the nine rune staves into the liquid. Stir the water at least nine times with the Ash/Yew twigs. Then as you are waiting for the swirling runes to settle, lay face down upon the ground. Cup you hands to your mouth and whilst still in contact with the earth (as if you were going to whisper into someone's ear) ask the earth mother your question or state what guidance you seek from her. When the liquid is still the runes will reveal her answer!

Hand-Fasting

Many couples today go through a "so called" Christianised form of marriage. They do so without really knowing the origins behind such ceremonies and the popular and altogether wrong assumptions that have been formed over the last few hundred years are such that contemporary weddings of today (being performed for the most part by Christian clergy) are, and have been the "norm" since the year dot! This view, that has been sold to the public as the way things have always been, is a gross misconception, the Pagan or heathen forms of wedding/handfasting are certainly not as alien to the modern day marriage as some may like us to think!

Slowly and thankfully the tide has now turned and what was once frowned upon by the people at large through bigotry and misinformation is now bouncing back from our Pagan past. The joyous and positive loving ceremonies performed by our distant ancestors can be shared once more by their kith and kin, maintaining the link to our history and Pagan heritage.

In 1753 one Lord Harwick decided to bring into being a "marriage act" up until this point in time and for hundreds of years before the "norm" for everyone except kings and the very wealthy and well-to-do was to be "Hand-fasted" by Pagan Priests/Priestess's. The local cunning woman/man (Lybläc) or Witch was the chosen figure to conduct and over-see the hand-fasting ritual. The Church had no interest whatsoever up until that time in the common man's Pagan practice of "tying the knot" but as I suspect there just may have been a little money to be made from those using the church and state for the regulation of marriage?

Let's take some things that happen during contemporary weddings of to day that the majority of folk may wonder why they are there and see where their origins begin.

The tiered wedding cake

In Anglo-Saxon times the handmaidens would place small cakes on top of each other until they formed a large pyramid shape. If the happy couple could successfully eat the top cake together (without using their hands) they would have a good and very prosperous married life.

Cutting the cake

Again at that time the groom would hand over his sword to his bride stating that it was an inheritance for the sons that she would bare him. She in turn would give back the blade saying that he needed it to protect her and any offspring that one day would inherit the weapon. Both holding the sword they would cut a cake; one half for him for the strength to defend and one half for her for the nourishment to conceive.

Tying the knot (wedding rings)

The couple to be handfasted would stand in front of each other holding hands, right hand to right hand and left hand to left in a figure of eight fashion. Their hands would have been tied together to form a perpetual never-ending knot which in turn was a representation of the sun and moon the two spheres bringing together the male and female energies the powers that ruled the heavens and rode the skies. This symbol of heavenly love eventually became symbolised by the groom splitting a ring, the lady wearing it about her neck showing her intent and loyalty to her man which in turn became the exchanging of rings (the figure of eight) that is widely used today.

Engagement
The period of a hand-fasting is a year and a day or thirteen moons. The origins of the engagement, for after this initial period the couple could make more solid and binding vows before the whole village or if their love was not as strong they could go their separate ways.

An interesting fact is that when the Marriage Act came into being in England the fact that in the north the law had not changed drove couples to travel across the border to Gretna Green in Scotland to get handfasted. This is the origin of eloping to Gretna Green.

Honeymoon
For a period of one month the happy couple would drink mead made of the sweetest honey, they would move to somewhere more secluded and make love at every opportunity. Hence one month being one moon about 28 days, the moving for privacy and the mead makes the origins of the Honeymoon.

Wedding dress
The origins of the white wedding dress are only as old as the Victorian era in England (Roman women wore white) Couples in our Anglo-Saxon past would wear the best and most brightly coloured garments that they could find.

Lyblác Hand-fasting rite

The Hearth shall be affirmed and flowers and greenery laid about it. Nearby trees and bushes shall be adorned with colourful ribbons. Fruit shall be placed upon the altar. The bride should be lead to the hearth by her father. Male cousins and brothers should walk beside and behind her holding torches (this was also an ancient Celtic & Roman tradition).

The couple adorned with crowns of red and white ribbon interlaced with greenery and flowers shall enter and stand before the Altar. Both shall kneel with the Lyblaeca/Lybbestre standing behind them.

The horn is taken up and sounded three times then replaced back upon the altar.

Lyblaeca/Lybbestre:

Stands in the ᛉ position facing the altar and says:

"Mother, Father there are those who would join
In the bonds of love and marriage"

Lyblaeca/Lybbestre:

Still standing in the ᛉ position now calls the Gods:

"Woden,
father
Be among us.

Frigg,
Holy Wife
We await your bounty.

Thunar, Brother
Ward this stead

Geofon, Sister
Bestow your presence upon us

Honoured ancestors
Let us all live and love once more
In the embrace of Erca and of our kin".

At this point, all assembled shall rejoice loudly.

Now touching firstly the groom on his right shoulder say:

[Groom's name] *Son of the earth and the hunters axe.*

What is your intent?

Groom answers:

I wish to be joined to my hearts delight.

Lyblaeca/Lybbestre:

And is this of your own free will.

[Groom] *It is my will.*

Lyblaeca/Lybbestre:

Placing the left hand upon the shoulder of the bride Lyblaeca/Lybbestre says:

[Bride's name] *Daughter of the heavens and the mysteries of Life*

What is your intent?

Bride answers:

I wish to be joined to my heart's delight.

Lyblaeca/Lybbestre:

And is this of your own free will.

[Bride] *It is my will.*

The bride and Groom stand turning to face the centre of the hearth the Lyblaeca/Lybbestre standing behind them says:

"Is this the true choice of you both?"

To which they both should reply:

"Yes this choice we have made"

Lyblaeca/Lybbestre:

Now stands between them and taking the right hand of the groom places it together with the right hand of the bride saying:

"That you are both of one mind is the start of your journey".

Lyblaeca/Lybbestre:

Now the couple should face each other and the Lyblaeca/ Lybbestre should take hold of the left hand of the bride placing it together with the left hand of the groom saying:

"Sometimes you shall not be of one mind?
So does this not break the bonds of the everlasting?"

The Lyblaeca/Lybbestre now takes the right hand of the bride placing it together with the right hand of the groom then says:

"At those times you shall remember how your wills can be as one, and then the light of your lives shall enter you both and you shall live and you shall love and the Gods shall smile upon you".

The hands of the couple now in a figure of 8 are bound and finished with three knots.

Lyblaeca/Lybbestre says:

"It is time to declare your love and intent amongst friends, before your kin and before your Gods". (The last knot finished on the word Gods as above)

Turning to the groom says: "cite these words".

"*I am,* ....(Name)...., *son of,*....(Father's name) ....*son of* (Mother's name)...., *and the family,* ....(Surname).... *The road of Love, Life and of the Gods has guided me here. I have found that which is ever precious, a friend, a lover and the purpose of all my desire. I pledge this day my Love and honour to thee,* .... (Bride's name)...., *I shall comfort and shelter you in the depths of harsh winter. I shall Love and cherish you in the quickening of the bud. I will share all that I have as the leaves turn in autumn and our bodies shall entwine under the warm golden sun. My life is yours as there can be no other. My shield and protection to weather any storm. A binding and bonding and sharing of all pleasure, for you are my passion and keeper of my heart".*

Now turning to the bride says: "cite these words".

"*I am,* ....(Name)...., *daughter of,*....(Father's name) ....*daughter of* (Mother's name)...., *and the family,* ....(Surname).... *The road of Love, Life and of the Gods has guided me here. I have found that which is ever precious, a friend, a lover and the purpose of all my desire. I pledge this day my Love and honour to thee, ...* (Groom's name)...., *I shall comfort and shelter you in the depths of harsh winter. I shall Love and cherish you in the quickening of the bud. I will share all that I have as the leaves turn in autumn and our bodies shall entwine under the warm golden sun. My life is yours as there can be no other. My comfort and support to weather any storm. A binding and bonding and sharing of all pleasure, for you are my champion and keeper of my heart".*

The couple's hands are untied and then the groom's right hand and the bride's left hand are re-tied. They are then lead to the northern point by the Lyblaeca/Lybbestre who stands behind them making the corresponding rune symbol with his seax over their heads and says:

(NORTH)

"Welga norðlic léoma
Ealdfæder
ìzas rún"

ᛁ

"Here before you stand those for witness
May they receive the gifts of the north".

Those who are to represent the elements at this point should pass over the gift.

The north should be something old, a family heirloom.

The east horse's tail or a feather.

The south a red candle (lit)

The west a small bottle of water (some of which is to be sprinkled over the couple).

The Earth is a seed and a bud (handed over by the Lyblaeca/Lybbestre the seed to the groom and the bud to the bride). All three bow their heads after each gift.

Now turning to the east, south then west eventually standing back in the centre at the hearth.

(EAST)

"Welga eastwind
Ferhðland
Ehwaz rún"

ᛖ

"Here before you stand those for witness
May they receive the gifts of the east".

(SOUTH)

"Welga brynebeorg
ælanland
Sigil rún"

ᛋ

"Here before you stand those for witness
May they receive the gifts of the south".

(WEST)

"Welga nâ bridel
gæbrecwaðum
Laguz rún"

ᛚ

"Here before you stand those for witness
May they receive the gifts of the west".

Now the couple should kneel at the centre of the hearth as the Lyblaeca/Lybbestre makes the rune sign over the hearth and says:

(EARTH)

"Welga eorthan mòdor
Nerthus
Gyfu rún"

X

"Here before you kneel those for witness
May they receive the gifts of the earth mother".

The couple now stands and the Lyblaeca/Lybbestre he/she takes the gifts one by one saying:

Ancestors give strength, hold creation and marvellous beauty
Air gives sky blessings and the sacredness of the mare
Fire gives passions heat and creates all life
Water gives the flowing of all language and the ear of the Gods
Earth gives comfort, bounty and worth.

And you both shall give of yourselves in the passing of the years
Mighty gifts, bestowed on those who are willing
This is your troth and the knot never ending
For all shall be taken should falseness declare.

Lyblaeca/Lybbestre:

Unties their hands and if rings are to be exchanged places the rings flat upon the groom's Seax/Sword. Now holding the blade with the rings placed upon them they are tipped into a small vessel full of milk and honey mixture. (The Celtic form is that the groom would drink the milk mixed with the blood of an Ox). The groom is now summoned to dip his hand into the bowl/vessel and find one of the rings (A good omen is for him to find the smaller bride's ring. This is quite easy to "arrange" for the success of good omen).

The groom now says (as he pulls out the ring):

"I have found you from the depths of all longing, as pale as milk and as sweet as honey do you accept me dearest heart?"

Bride says: "*I do*" and the groom puts the ring on her finger.

The bride now delves into the mixture pulling out the second larger ring and says:

"As I slept in the depths of all longing I awoke to your voice, together as one, we have laughed and lay my own beloved. Do you accept me?"

Groom says: "*I do*" The bride then places the ring upon his finger.

The groom now takes his Seax/sword and passes it to his bride saying:

"Wife, this blade has served me well; keep it in good stead for all our sons"

Bride takes the blade and passes it back to the groom saying:

"Husband, until such a time as our fine sons can hold, this blade is best served for our protection at your side".

They both hold the Seax/Sword and cut a small cake they link arms she eats one half and he eats the other.

Lyblaeca/Lybbestre says:

"Sustenance for the making of seed and sustenance for the bearing of fruit".

[Turning now to the bride and groom the Lyblaeca/Lybbestre says:]

May the Gods be forever with you
So you shall cherish the light of your grand children's eyes
The Gods secure your poorest days be of life's misfortunes
And your richest of blessings abound.

Then in a loud voice so that all attending can clearly hear:

"Today and before your Gods you have pledged your troth. You are now man and wife. If you stay true in respect, honour, strength and love then no matter what comes know this, you are nevermore alone. And further more as the years move ever onward you shall grow and be a beacon for all to witness. So now kiss and make merry for the Honeymoon has begun".

At this stage all present shall make loud rejoicing and toasts to the happy couple. (This ensures that any evil spirits lurking at the edges shall be dispersed).

Now follows the Cakes and Ale. After which music and merry-making is shall be the order of the day. Maidens shall pile up the cakes to see if the happy couple can eat the topmost cake (without hands). The couple should as a rule drink mead at this time. The hearth should be sealed after this short merriment. The Lyblaeca/Lybbestre should abstain from drinking until the hearth has been sealed. Then the party can begin.

At this point the bride and groom each take a lock of their hair and proceed to bind the hair together with red cord/ribbon. After this has been done and away from the main party a square of turf should be cut with the sword (only three sides of the square being cut to make a flap that should be opened revealing the earth. Also the turf can be cut beforehand by the Lyblaeca/Lybbestre so as to ease the cutting by the bride and groom.) The hair is then placed within a birch leaf (Which holds and maintains the couple's powers together) and places the parcel in the middle of the square upon the earth. The couple now take the milk and honey mixture tipping it together upon the "bletsian" (item to be blessed i.e.; hair, cord and leaf) saying a prayer to Erca the earth goddess for good fortune and fertility. After which the turf should be replaced, patted down and left to grow back as it was before.

Acknowledgments/ Bibliography

Leechcraft. Stephen Pollington. Published by Anglo Saxon Books.

The Tree. The Complete book of Saxon Witchcraft. Raymond Buckland. Published by Weiser Books.

Wordcraft. New English to Old English dictionary & Thesaurus. Stephen Pollington. Published by Anglo Saxon Books.

Rudiments of Runelore. Stephen Pollington. Published by Anglo Saxon Books.

Germania. The Agrigola and the Germania. Tacitus, Cornelius. Published by Harmonsworth/Penguin

Anglo Saxon Verse, Charms, Maxims and Heroic Legends L. J. Rodrigues. Published by Pinner

Lost Gods of England. Kathleen Herbert. Published by Anglo Saxon Books.

Some Other titles from Capall Bann

Heathen Paths - Viking and Anglo Saxon Pagan Beliefs

by Pete Jennings

This book is written from a different perspective to other books published on aspects of The Northern Tradition to present a handbook of accumulated data so that people can read and interpret it for themselves, aided by sometimes conflicting or complementary opinions clearly labelled, enabling the reader to develop and adapt their own theories and practices, rather than have them laid out. Where possible Pete compares more than one source of information. Trying to subjectively observe a movement from within, whilst being a part of it oneself is a delicate path to tread, but in this book Pete does an admirable job, separating them from the historical data being presented. "*This book is not a how-to manual filled with rituals, although there are some ideas and a sample Blot at the end of the book to get you creating your own from the material you have read.... this book certainly brings you closer to the way things were seen and done in those times.... I enjoyed this book immensely, I can see that in some sections where the author talks about his conclusions, they could be contentious for some readers, but that is also what makes the book great – it makes you think. I can certainly imagine Heathens sitting down at a pub discussing this book, and it causing some great debates!*" *Pentacle* magazine ISBN 186163286X £14.95

Asyniur - Women's Mysteries in the Northern Tradition

by Sheena McGrath

"excellent. Well researched and well balanced...scrupulous honesty...she is clearly a writer to watch out for in future...highly recommended" White Dragon

Unlike other titles in this area, this book looks at all aspects of women's lives, their magic and their religion in the Northern Tradition. Topics covered include the nature of women's activities from the 'traditional' position of housewife to those of scald and warrior, the role of female figures in creation and Ragnarok myths, a comprehensive coverage of Northern Tradition Goddesses, rituals specific to women, runes and the female power of foreseeing events, Seidr - the combination of witchcraft and shamanism, its connections with Freya as well as the connections between her, fertility magic and Seidr itself. ISBN 186163 004 2 £10.95

The Book of Seiðr - The Native English and Northern European Shamanic Tradition **by Runic John**

Seiðr is the ancient Northern European shamanism. The main practice of seiðr, as with all shamanic traditions, is the use of various extremely ancient techniques to affect the mind and alter our consciousness to a state in which we can perceive and work with the hidden realm of spirit directly. We can use seidr to connect on a deeper level to our own inner self and to enhance our particular skills and positive qualities. Seiðr can also help us to connect to the hidden realms of nature on a before unimaginable depth, allowing us to gain an experiential understanding of the natural world and all that dwell therein; to actually feel one with the forest, the earth and the sky. Through seiðr you may truly form a real relationship with our ancestors and the elder gods and goddesses of our folk. As you embark on this path of seiðr, never again will the world look empty and hollow, for your eyes will learn to see the spirit in all things and to hear the voices of the ancient ones. ISBN 186163 2290 £14.95

FREE DETAILED CATALOGUE

Capall Bann is owned and run by people actively involved in many of the areas in which we publish. A detailed illustrated catalogue is available on request, SAE or International Postal Coupon appreciated. **Titles can be ordered direct from Capall Bann, post free in the UK** (cheque or PO with order) or from good bookshops and specialist outlets.

A Breath Behind Time, Terri Hector
A Soul is Born by Eleyna Williamson
Angels and Goddesses - Celtic Christianity & Paganism, M. Howard
The Art of Conversation With the Genius Loci, Barry Patterson
Arthur - The Legend Unveiled, C Johnson & E Lung
Astrology The Inner Eye - A Guide in Everyday Language, E Smith
Auguries and Omens - The Magical Lore of Birds, Yvonne Aburrow
Asyniur - Women's Mysteries in the Northern Tradition, S McGrath
Beginnings - Geomancy, Builder's Rites & Electional Astrology in the European Tradition, Nigel Pennick
Between Earth and Sky, Julia Day
The Book of Seidr, Runic John
Caer Sidhe - Celtic Astrology and Astronomy, Michael Bayley
Call of the Horned Piper, Nigel Jackson
Can't Sleep, Won't Sleep, Linda Louisa Dell
Carnival of the Animals, Gregor Lamb
Cat's Company, Ann Walker
Celebrating Nature, Gordon MacLellan
Celtic Faery Shamanism, Catrin James
Celtic Faery Shamanism - The Wisdom of the Otherworld, Catrin James
Celtic Lore & Druidic Ritual, Rhiannon Ryall
Celtic Sacrifice - Pre Christian Ritual & Religion, Marion Pearce
Celtic Saints and the Glastonbury Zodiac, Mary Caine
Circle and the Square, Jack Gale
Come Back To Life, Jenny Smedley
Company of Heaven, Jan McDonald
Compleat Vampyre - The Vampyre Shaman, Nigel Jackson
Cottage Witchcraft, Jan McDonald
Creating Form From the Mist - The Wisdom of Women in Celtic Myth and Culture, Lynne Sinclair-Wood
Crystal Clear - A Guide to Quartz Crystal, Jennifer Dent
Crystal Doorways, Simon & Sue Lilly
Crossing the Borderlines - Guising, Masking & Ritual Animal Disguise in the

European Tradition, Nigel Pennick
Dragons of the West, Nigel Pennick
Earth Dance - A Year of Pagan Rituals, Jan Brodie
Earth Harmony - Places of Power, Holiness & Healing, Nigel Pennick
Earth Magic, Margaret McArthur
Egyptian Animals - Guardians & Gateways of the Gods, Akkadia Ford
Eildon Tree (The) Romany Language & Lore, Michael Hoadley
Enchanted Forest - The Magical Lore of Trees, Yvonne Aburrow
Eternal Priestess, Sage Weston
Eternally Yours Faithfully, Roy Radford & Evelyn Gregory
Everything You Always Wanted To Know About Your Body, But So Far Nobody's Been Able To Tell You, Chris Thomas & D Baker
Experiencing the Green Man, Rob Hardy & Teresa Moorey
Face of the Deep - Healing Body & Soul, Penny Allen
Fairies and Nature Spirits, Teresa Moorey
Fairies in the Irish Tradition, Molly Gowen
Familiars - Animal Powers of Britain, Anna Franklin
Flower Wisdom, Katherine Kear
Fool's First Steps, (The) Chris Thomas
Forest Paths - Tree Divination, Brian Harrison, Ill. S. Rouse
From Past to Future Life, Dr Roger Webber
From Stagecraft To Witchcraft, , Patricia Crowther
Gardening For Wildlife Ron Wilson
God Year, The, Nigel Pennick & Helen Field
Goddess on the Cross, Dr George Young
Goddess Year, The, Nigel Pennick & Helen Field
Goddesses, Guardians & Groves, Jack Gale
Handbook For Pagan Healers, Liz Joan
Handbook of Fairies, Ronan Coghlan
Healing Book, The, Chris Thomas and Diane Baker
Healing Homes, Jennifer Dent
Healing Journeys, Paul Williamson
Healing Stones, Sue Philips
Heathen Paths - Viking and Anglo Saxon Beliefs by Pete Jennings
Herb Craft - Shamanic & Ritual Use of Herbs, Lavender & Franklin
Hidden Heritage - Exploring Ancient Essex, Terry Johnson
Hub of the Wheel, Skytoucher
In and Out the Windows, Dilys Gator
In Search of Herne the Hunter, Eric Fitch
In Search of the Green Man, Peter Hill
Inner Celtia, Alan Richardson & David Annwn
Inner Mysteries of the Goths, Nigel Pennick
Inner Space Workbook - Develop Through Tarot, Cat Summers & Julian Vayne
In Search of Pagan Gods, Teresa Moorey
Intuitive Journey, Ann Walker Isis - African Queen, Akkadia Ford
Journey Home, The, Chris Thomas

Kecks, Keddles & Kesh - Celtic Lang & The Cog Almanac, Bayley
Language of the Psycards, Berenice
Legend of Robin Hood, The, Richard Rutherford-Moore
Lid Off the Cauldron, Patricia Crowther
Light From the Shadows - Modern Traditional Witchcraft, Gwyn
Living Tarot, Ann Walker
Lore of the Sacred Horse, Marion Davies
Lost Lands & Sunken Cities (2nd ed.), Nigel Pennick
Lyblác, Anglo Saxon Witchcraft by Wulfeage
The Magic and Mystery of Trees, Teresa Moorey
Magic For the Next 1,000 Years, Jack Gale
Magic of Herbs - A Complete Home Herbal, Rhiannon Ryall
Magical Guardians - Exploring the Spirit and Nature of Trees, Philip Heselton
Magical History of the Horse, Janet Farrar & Virginia Russell
Magical Lore of Animals, Yvonne Aburrow
Magical Lore of Cats, Marion Davies
Magical Lore of Herbs, Marion Davies
Magick Without Peers, Ariadne Rainbird & David Rankine
Masks of Misrule - Horned God & His Cult in Europe, Nigel Jackson
Medicine For The Coming Age, Lisa Sand MD
Medium Rare - Reminiscences of a Clairvoyant, Muriel Renard
Menopausal Woman on the Run, Jaki da Costa
Mind Massage - 60 Creative Visualisations, Marlene Maundrill
Mirrors of Magic - Evoking the Spirit of the Dewponds, P Heselton
The Moon and You, Teresa Moorey
Moon Mysteries, Jan Brodie
Mysteries of the Runes, Michael Howard
Mystic Life of Animals, Ann Walker
New Celtic Oracle The, Nigel Pennick & Nigel Jackson
Oracle of Geomancy, Nigel Pennick
Pagan Feasts - Seasonal Food for the 8 Festivals, Franklin & Phillips
Paganism For Teens, Jess Wynne
Patchwork of Magic - Living in a Pagan World, Julia Day
Pathworking - A Practical Book of Guided Meditations, Pete Jennings
Personal Power, Anna Franklin
Pickingill Papers - The Origins of Gardnerian Wicca, Bill Liddell
Pillars of Tubal Cain, Nigel Jackson
Places of Pilgrimage and Healing, Adrian Cooper
Planet Earth - The Universe's Experiment, Chris Thomas
Practical Divining, Richard Foord
Practical Meditation, Steve Hounsome
Practical Spirituality, Steve Hounsome
Psychic Self Defence - Real Solutions, Jan Brodie
Real Fairies, David Tame
Reality - How It Works & Why It Mostly Doesn't, Rik Dent
Romany Tapestry, Michael Houghton

Runic Astrology, Nigel Pennick
Sacred Animals, Gordon MacLellan
Sacred Celtic Animals, Marion Davies, Ill. Simon Rouse
Sacred Dorset - On the Path of the Dragon, Peter Knight
Sacred Grove - The Mysteries of the Forest, Yvonne Aburrow
Sacred Geometry, Nigel Pennick
Sacred Nature, Ancient Wisdom & Modern Meanings, A Cooper
Sacred Ring - Pagan Origins of British Folk Festivals, M. Howard
Season of Sorcery - On Becoming a Wisewoman, Poppy Palin
Seasonal Magic - Diary of a Village Witch, Paddy Slade
Secret Places of the Goddess, Philip Heselton
Secret Signs & Sigils, Nigel Pennick
The Secrets of East Anglian Magic, Nigel Pennick
A Seeker's Guide To Past Lives, Paul Williamson
Seeking Pagan Gods, Teresa Moorey
A Seer's Guide To Crystal Divination, Gale Halloran
Self Enlightenment, Mayan O'Brien
Soul Resurgence, Poppy Palin
Spirits of the Air, Jaq D Hawkins
Spirits of the Water, Jaq D Hawkins
Spirits of the Fire, Jaq D Hawkins
Spirits of the Aether, Jaq D Hawkins
Spirits of the Earth, Jaq D Hawkins
Stony Gaze, Investigating Celtic Heads John Billingsley
Stumbling Through the Undergrowth , Mark Kirwan-Heyhoe
Subterranean Kingdom, The, revised 2nd ed, Nigel Pennick
Symbols of Ancient Gods, Rhiannon Ryall
Talking to the Earth, Gordon MacLellan
Talking With Nature, Julie Hood
Taming the Wolf - Full Moon Meditations, Steve Hounsome
Teachings of the Wisewomen, Rhiannon Ryall
The Other Kingdoms Speak, Helena Hawley
Transformation of Housework, Ben Bushill
Tree: Essence of Healing, Simon & Sue Lilly
Tree: Essence, Spirit & Teacher, Simon & Sue Lilly
Tree Seer, Simon & Sue Lilly
Torch and the Spear, Patrick Regan
Understanding Chaos Magic, Jaq D Hawkins
Understanding Past Lives, Dilys Gater
Understanding Second Sight, Dilys Gater
Understanding Spirit Guides, Dilys Gater
Understanding Star Children, Dilys Gater
The Urban Shaman, Dilys Gater
Vortex - The End of History, Mary Russell
Warp and Weft - In Search of the I-Ching, William de Fancourt
Warriors at the Edge of Time, Jan Fry

Water Witches, Tony Steele
Way of the Magus, Michael Howard
Weaving a Web of Magic, Rhiannon Ryall
West Country Wicca, Rhiannon Ryall
What's Your Poison? vol 1, Tina Tarrant
Wheel of the Year, Teresa Moorey & Jane Brideson
Wildwitch - The Craft of the Natural Psychic, Poppy Palin
Wildwood King , Philip Kane
A Wisewoman's Book of Tea Leaf Reading, Pat Barki
The Witching Path, Moira Stirland
The Witch's Kitchen, Val Thomas
The Witches' Heart, Eileen Smith
Treading the Mill - Practical CraftWorking in Modern Traditional Witchcraft by Nigel Pearson
Witches of Oz, Matthew & Julia Philips
Witchcraft Myth Magic Mystery and... Not Forgetting Fairies, Ralph Harvey
Wondrous Land - The Faery Faith of Ireland by Dr Kay Mullin
Working With Crystals, Shirley o'Donoghue
Working With Natural Energy, Shirley o'Donoghue
Working With the Merlin, Geoff Hughes
Your Talking Pet, Ann Walker
The Zodiac Experience, Patricia Crowther

FREE detailed catalogue

Contact: Capall Bann Publishing, Auton Farm, Milverton, Somerset, TA4 1NE